Unleash the Wise Leader in You!
A Woman's Guide to Leadership
Donna Marino, PsyD

*Francine,
May you make
your mark on
the world!
♥ Dr. Donna*

Copyright 2020; Donna Marino, PsyD, Ltd

Dedication

To My Husband, Matt Dahl, without whom this book would not have been possible.
To My Children, Ella, and Isabelle, who inspire me to be a Wise Leader in all that I do.
To My Mother, Mary Marino, for all the sacrifices you have made for me.
To My Father, Lester Marino, and My Sister, Mary Ellen Marino, who are my WHY.

And lastly for the Notorious RBG who suddenly passed just as this book was coming out.
You have changed our lives profoundly. We are your legacy.
Without the Honorable Justice Ruth Bader Ginsburg paving the way, this book may
have never been written. Thank you. You are already missed.

Table of Contents

Introduction: My Why: How the Power of Purpose Wrote this Book 4

Author's Note 8

Part I: The 5 Principles of Wise Leadership 9

    Chapter 1: Claim Your Leadership 10

    Chapter 2: Unleash Your Ambition 16

    Chapter 3: Find Your Voice 25

    Chapter 4: Lift Each Other Up 31

    Chapter 5: The Power of Purpose 36

Part II: Overcoming the Obstacles to Your Success 39

    Introduction 40

    Chapter 6: The Boogey Man (aka Fear) 41

    Chapter 7: Imposter Syndrome (Self-Worth & Self-Doubt) 48

    Chapter 8: Time & Money (Scarcity Mindset) 55

    Chapter 9: Sabotage (Bucking the Status Quo, and Homeostasis) 58

    Chapter 10: Your Tribe (or lack of) 62

Part III: Implementation: What does this look like in real life? 68

    Introduction 69

    Chapter 11: At Home 70

    Chapter 12: At Work 77

    Chapter 13: In Your Community 84

    Chapter 14: In the World 90

    Chapter 15: Why you need to put this book into action NOW 95

Introduction

On October 6, 2017, I came home, rushing in the door from work. It was a Friday, and I had that Friday excitement. My kids were going to their dad's house for the weekend, and I was excited for "date night" with my husband. Martinis, and sushi. Yum. It had been a good day at work, and I was feeling great. I was the Clinical, and Psychology Department Manager of a large, multiple-location, mental health practice that served our community, and over 4000 people. I wore a lot of hats running the Continuing Education department: Maintaining its certifications, overseeing all of the psychology department needs, including training, the post-doctoral program, hiring, supervision, etc. I also provided training, management, and supervision over the Clinical Supervisors, and their staff while also overseeing, writing, and implementing all of our policies, and procedures, and ensuring both productivity, and quality services. Like I said, a lot of hats. It could be very stressful, but I loved my team, and the people with whom I worked. This Friday had been an especially good day, and Fridays always had a special energy to them.

So, I flung open the door. I had left work late, again, and missed the kids before they left for their dad's house. My husband was in the kitchen, and I was shouting as I came in from the garage, "Hey! It's Friday! Where do you want to go? I'm ready!" He walked out from the kitchen, coming around the corner, and asked me to sit down. Never a good sign. I knew that something was wrong. Unfortunately, I am not a newbie to bad news. Bad news seems to run in my family …but that's another book. My head went quickly to the task of imagining what it could be. I assumed it was something work-related, and maybe he had been let go.

I asked, "Is everything okay?" He said "no", and repeated, "please sit down." I sat down on the couch, and he sat down on the large ottoman across from me. He looked me in the eyes with his hands folded in front of him, took a deep breath, and said, "Your sister…expired."

It took me a while to process what he was saying. "Expired?" What did that even mean? What was he even saying? It started to settle in. My jaw dropped open, but no sound came out. My hand went up over my mouth to cover it, but still nothing. My husband went on.

"I got a call from your brother, Chris, earlier. He got a call from your mom. Apparently, Mary Ellen didn't show up for work today. When she didn't show, they called her boyfriend. He was out of town and called your Mom. Your Mom went over to her apartment and found her…she was lying on the floor of her bathroom. She appeared to have been there for a while…she was purple."

I was quiet for a long time. I was in shock; I couldn't make a sound; I couldn't process. My sister had just celebrated her 40th birthday. She had had a big party just the weekend before. I hadn't gone. It was in New York. I lived in Chicago. I had too much work to do; I needed to be with my family; I didn't have the time or money. ...excuses. She looked so happy in the pictures. What had happened?

Nobody knew. An autopsy would be performed. As far as we knew, her boyfriend was the last one to speak to her on Wednesday night. We couldn't get into her phone or computer. No one knew the passwords.

My husband finally asked me to say something so he would know that I wasn't catatonic. I could barely whisper the words, "I don't know what to say." I could scarcely squeak them out. Then somewhere between that silence on the couch, and walking upstairs to my room to change my clothes, came the wailing. ...the guttural, primal wailing with loud sobs, and screaming that comes from the deepest parts of you. I began to yell, "No!" over, and over, and over. "No! No! No!" I banged on the wall in my closet with my fist while I yelled, wailed, and sobbed. This could not be happening. Not my younger sister. Not my best friend. We lost our dad years ago in the attacks on the WTC on 9-11. I was not a novice to sudden, tragic death, but one per family was enough, right? This couldn't be happening again.

Months later, we would get the autopsy report back...accidental overdose. I looked up everything online that I could find, reviewed the medical examiner's report. I read the diary that my mother had found. This was no accident. Maybe she didn't intend, exactly, for it to happen at that moment. Maybe she was just playing Russian Roulette with alcohol, and medication. Maybe she just didn't know that this time, it would work. Her diary was full of suicidal thoughts and plans for months before that day.

In fact, she had reached out to me the August before we lost her. She told me that she had been depressed for a year wishing every night that she would not wake up in the morning. I gave her names of therapists, and workbooks she could use. I asked my brother to keep an eye on her, but I wasn't specific. I didn't want to betray her trust. I didn't want her to stop telling me things or alarm anyone. She had had chronic suicidal thoughts for most of our lives. I never thought she would really act. I wish I had done more.

So, why am I telling you this story now? ...and what in the world does this have to do with Wise Leadership for Women anyway? How is this all connected?

When I lost my father in 9-11, I just knew that I was called to honor his memory by doing good work in the world and helping others through their own traumas and tragedies. I was to lead by example of how you can experience the worst tragedy, and still choose positivity, love, and caring for others. I was to help others.

Well, when I lost Mary Ellen, it threw my world upside down. It was a wake-up call. Sure, I was unhappy because I was grieving, but I also realized that while I had a great title, lots of responsibility, and a nice income in my career, I was not being a Wise Leader. I was not doing the work that really lit me up. I was not serving those that needed my guidance most. I wasn't really serving my values or my zone of genius. What I *was* doing was over-working, over-stressing, and not being present to my family because I couldn't shut my brain off. I wasn't taking care of myself. I was burnt out, severely.

So, I quit my job.

In a professional manner, of course. But three months after Mary Ellen passed, I took a leap of faith and gave my 30-day notice.

Life was too short to miss out on my family or to not answer my calling. I realized how run down I was, how I was wasting precious time being in the wrong place. I realized how out of alignment I had become with my own values, with my own purpose; something I had coached many others on before. I needed to course-correct, to walk the walk, and to empower women to share their gifts and talents with the world. I felt like I hadn't done enough with Mary Ellen. I didn't want that to happen again. I wanted to help women rise up and step into their greatness.

So, I chose to become a Wise Leader, first by leaving my job. Then by healing myself and finally by creating a business that helps others unleash their inner Wise Leader so that each and every one of us can make the contributions that we are called to, but especially women.

I write this book to inspire women to Unleash Your Wise Leader. I write this book at a time where women make up less than 5% of the leaders in Fortune 500 companies, and where women's rights have come under attack again politically, and socially.

Now, this book is not about eliminating male leadership. It is about bringing balance and diversity to the table. It is about women making their contributions and taking their seats at the leadership table. It's our time ladies. No more waiting for someone to make room for you or to bestow some title on you. You have to claim it! You have to own it! It starts with you.

In Part One, this book will take you through the five main principles of Wise Leadership, and why each one is important. In Part Two, we will address the obstacles that get in the way of becoming a Wise Leader and implementing these principles. Finally, in Part Three, you will learn how to show up as the Wise Leader at home, at work, and in the world. What does it look like when you live the principles, clear your blocks, and begin to be a Wise Leader with a big impact? You'll find out here.

As a special bonus, each chapter has its own exercises for embodying the principles, clearing the obstacles that get in the way, and bringing your work out into the world.. You can download the accompanying audio tracks of guided meditation, visualization, and hypnosis at www.drdonnamarino.com/unleash to begin implementing these practices right away, and begin clearing the blocks to your success.

I want to leave you with this.

Please, Be Bold. Please, allow yourself to be Fabulous. Dare to be Brilliant. ...and Share Your Light with the World ...Because We are ALL Waiting for You!
Love,
Dr. Donna

Author's Notes

An Important Word about Gender

In today's complex world and the always-changing advancement in our understanding of others, I recognize that the world is no longer viewed in two genders: male or female. I understand that terms are changing, identities are changing, and that the understanding we have today will likely be different by the time you are holding this book in your hand. I mean no disrespect by relying on the terms male, female, man, woman, etc. Please read this book through your own lens, as it applies to you. Please know that while I have written this book specifically with women in mind, I believe that the Wise Leadership principles can apply to everyone, but especially to all of those who are under-represented in leadership, whether that is about race, ethnicity, religion, gender, sexuality, etc. Please take what you like, and leave the rest. On that note, let's talk about how you can get the most out of this book.

How to get the most out of this book

The way to get the most out of this book is to actually **DO** each of the exercises within it. There will be action steps along the way, as well as audio recordings to help you embody the Wise Leader. It is not enough to know something. We all know lots of things, but unless you are living it, unless you are genuinely embodying it, you don't really know it. Keeping it in your head will not do you or anyone else any good. You have to live it. So be brave, take the time, and do the work. You will need a notebook or journal to do the exercises in this book or you can purchase the companion workbook which has all of the exercises from this book, just waiting for you to complete!

Part I: The Five Principles of Wise Leadership

Chapter One: Claim Your Leadership

So, I know right now, just reading that title, there are two groups of people reading that. One is saying, duh, "I've already done that," and the other is saying, "But I'm not a leader." So to the first response, I say, maybe you have, and maybe you just think you have. Keep an open mind, and let's explore. But even if you have already claimed your leadership, stick around; there is something in here for you too, I promise. ...and for the latter, I am going to prove to you that you are! So let's begin!

Are You A Leader?

You would be surprised how few women actually raise their hands when I ask, are you a leader?

Picture it. ...I'm standing in front of a group of all women who are attending the Women's Health and Wealth Summit on a snowy day in April in Chicago (yes, sometimes we still get snow in April ...late April). These women come from all tracks of life but include business owners, doctors, lawyers, women who work in the financial industry; in other words: Successful, driven women. Yet, when I ask the question, who here sees themselves as a leader, hardly anyone raises their hand.

Yet, when I begin to reframe and ask questions like, "who here is a business owner?" or "who here serves on the PTA/PTO" or "who here is a mom?" the hands begin to fly up. So, I have to say, "Well, guess what, ladies? All of these roles require leadership. So if you are raising your hand to any one of these questions, you are a leader."

I wish I could say that this is the only group this has happened with, but it has happened over, and over, and over again. Maybe we need the definition of leadership for answers.

My favorite definition of leadership comes from John Quincy Adams, who said:

"If your actions inspire others to dream more, learn more, do more, and become more, you are a leader."

Look at that, ladies. It turns out you are all leaders. You are already leading: in your homes with your children and partners, in your communities in your churches, synagogues, schools, scouts, at work, as a business owner, manager, team leader, service provider, executive (of course), etc. You are leading everywhere you go.

But you can't claim it unless you own it first. What's the difference? Owning it is acknowledging it, saying yes. Claiming it is putting your stake in the ground. Ladies, you can't wait for someone to bestow the word leader upon you. I know you are a high achieving woman, and when you were in school, you loved A's on tests, making the Dean's list, and graduating summa cum laude. You love the ribbons, the prizes, the trophies that validate and acknowledge you. But there is no trophy for leadership. Unless you're Richard Branson, Sting, or that Dyson guy, you probably aren't getting knighted by the Queen. Are there any women who are? (Turns out women become Dames instead Knights; Knights are reserved for men only, and yes, Judy Dench and Helen Mirren have been Dame-d). Anyway, if you are waiting for someone to decide for you, just stop. You have to decide.

Action Step #1

Go ahead and get your journal or Wise Leader Workbook. Stop for a minute, and just think about all of the areas in your life that you are already leading. Write them down. Write down everywhere that you influence and/or inspire others. It is important for you to see it in black and white right in front of you, so don't skip this step. Go ahead, and write it down, everywhere you are currently leading, even those of you who already identify as leaders should do this, because you are probably leading in ways that come so naturally to you that you don't even realize that you are leading even more than you already thought.

Okay, so now that you have your list, take a picture of it with your phone, so you always have it with you. So that, in those times of insecurity and self-doubt (which we will dive into deeper in Part II), you will have it with you at all times to refer back to, to remind yourself of the leader that you really are.

Why Aren't You Claiming Your Leadership

Why is it hard for women, in particular, to Claim Their Leadership? Although some men can also have issues with this, it is much more common among women. Now I've already hit on one.

Many of you are waiting for someone to decide for you. You are waiting for that promotion that moves you into a leadership position, you are waiting to receive a certain title, or hit a certain income level, or you think that being a SAHM doesn't make you a leader. You think "I'll know I am a leader when [insert external validation here]." Now that you know that that is just BS, what are the other reasons holding you back from Claiming your Leadership?

Let's start with our biology.

It starts with our early conditioning in our childhood. Now, I know many of us are raising our own sons and daughters differently, and I hope that we see a cultural shift in this in the upcoming decades; however, the obsequious messaging has been that women are to be submissive, people-pleasing, codependent, and more concerned with others than themselves (wait that last one sounds like leadership...in Part III we will talk about how to use this feminine trait to your advantage in leadership). Women are more likely to put themselves on the back-burner, to give others credit than themselves, and to minimize their gifts and talents. Girls are conditioned from an early age to be good, nice, thoughtful, giving, loving, obedient, responsible, kind, and humble. While boys are conditioned to be strong, ambitious, tough, risk-taking or adventurous, leaders, and providers.

In addition, women are also more likely to seek the approval and validation of others. How do we receive approval, and validation of others? By complying with others' beliefs of how we "should" be. Unfortunately, there is still a cultural consciousness of what it means to be a "good girl," and even if we consciously object to these ideas, they are still swimming in our subconscious mind and driving at least a portion of our behaviors.

Think about it. It wasn't that long ago that women stayed at home while men went to work. ...and despite the woman running all of the household duties, men were still seen as the "head of the household" or the "king of the castle." So again, even though women were leading at home, they were not even recognized as leaders of their own homes.

We are really not that far out from when it was unheard of for women to work outside of the home. Working outside of the home, especially for married women, really only took root during World War II, and then many women did not continue working when their husbands came home. From an evolutionary standpoint, this is barely a nanosecond in time. Our consciousness is still catching up. So, while we have made great strides, there are still so many subtle, and not-so-subtle, messages about what a woman is and should be, and what roles she can and should play in the world.

Psychologist Alfred Adler said, belonging is the most basic need of all humans, and we will do whatever we believe is necessary to belong. So, if our subconscious or our conscious brain believes that being a good girl does not include being a leader, and being a good girl is necessary for belonging, we will not self-identify, even when we are already demonstrating those behaviors. We won't want to be seen in that light, and we will avoid it. We will keep working behind the scenes leading others, but not actually taking leadership credit.

Why is that so bad? Because it is disempowering for you, and for all women. It perpetuates the stereotypes of women. It limits our daughters and tells our sons that it's okay. It minimizes you and your accomplishments, and it sends a message to the world that women have less power, less control, less worth, and that others can make decisions for them. That is not okay.

But what about those of you who already believe you've claimed your leadership and are self-identifying as leaders. How do these subconscious beliefs show up for you? How are you still conforming to cultural ideas and seeking validation and approval? Well, think about this: Are you truly showing up in your leadership role as the full expression of yourself? Are you hiding parts of you that you think might not be approved of from your colleagues or higher-ups? Do you hold back in meetings? Allow yourself to be interrupted? Withhold innovative ideas because you aren't sure they will be accepted? Are you leading like yourself or mimicking your male counterparts, and how they lead? Do you worry about being too soft? Too bitchy? Too much? Have you applied for that next level, or are you waiting to be perfect before you do?

Action Step #2

Take the time now to write down your answers to these questions above, and to think about where you are still conforming to other's ideas of who you should be. Where have you been holding yourself back? What parts of you are you not expressing because they do not comply with cultural norms? Spend some time journaling on your own individual reasons that are holding you back from fully claiming your leadership and contemplate letting them go. Name it, Own it, Claim it.

You may not like this fact, but the truth is women are biologically hardwired to be caretakers. It is not just conditioning but it is actually in our DNA (just look at the research of David Buss and evolutionary psychology). It is hardwired into us for the survival of our species. ...and evolution is a slow, slow process. But that's okay; **because the idea that caretaking and leadership are opposites is just junk!**

Claiming Your Leadership does not mean that you can't be a caretaker or nurturing or warm or even feminine. It doesn't mean that we have to lead in the same way men do. In fact, it's better when we don't (also more on that in Part III). The leadership table needs a set of diverse ideas, approaches, and points of view. That's how we get innovation, inclusion, and growth. These things do not exist by having only like-minded people sit around the table and pat each other on the back, agreeing with each idea. Innovation and expansion or growth come from differing points of view that challenge one another and help reveal blind spots that can't be revealed when everyone has the same ones. Bottom line: Your unique feminine voice matters, and it matters more than you think. It's time to shatter our ideas of what leadership is and drill it down to its most basic concepts. Anytime you inspire, influence, guide, or direct others, you are acting as a leader.

So, are YOU ready to Claim Your Leadership?

Are you ready to declare that you are a leader right here, and now without anyone else's permission? Because this is where it all starts. It starts when you just go ahead and decide that you are a leader. Now is the time. There is nothing left to wait for. Just decide. Are you a leader or not?

Once you have decided you already are a leader (not going to be or someday, but now), I want you to stand for three minutes every day in Wonder Woman pose. Stand with your hands in fists on your hips, elbows out, feet at least hip-width apart, chin up, back straight, chest out. This comes from Amy Cuddy's work out of Harvard on power posing. Holding this pose for three minutes a day will help you embody the energy of being a leader. You must embody what you want to be, not just think it. Thinking is not enough. This is a whole-body experience.

Next, I want you to create your own leadership affirmation. Start with "I am" and then finish that sentence with what type of leader you want to be. "I am" is a powerful way to begin any affirmation. It brings it into the present tense and sends a message to your brain that this is a true fact about yourself, but you have to be able to believe it. People sometimes create affirmations that don't work because they are too far from how they really see themselves. If this is really hard for you, you might have to start with, "I am becoming a leader." But, if you are ready to be bolder, try something like, "I am a wise and confident leader" or "I am an empathic leader" or "I am a courageous leader." You get to decide, first to be a leader, and then what kind of leader you want to be.

Once you've created your affirmation, write it down somewhere where you will see it every day, like on a post-it note on your bathroom mirror or on your computer monitor or laptop. Then, say it out loud every day while looking in the mirror. Hear yourself say it. Declare it. If you are really daring, yell it loudly at the top of your lungs once a day. Again, we are learning to embody being a leader. These physical actions help us move it from a thought to a level of embodiment.

Want more ways to claim and embody your leadership?

- Write your own leadership mission statement

- Write your own leadership job description

- Write your 'leader archetype.' Write a clear description of who you are as a leader. How do you walk, talk, dress? Who do you associate with? Where do you eat, shop, vacation? Who is this person, you, the leader?

- Begin implementing your mission, job description, and archetype in all that you do.

- Place things in your environment that make you feel like a leader.

- Take time each day to visualize yourself in this way.

- For a guided visualization to help you Claim Your Leadership go to www.drdonnamarino.com/unleash

Chapter Two: Unleash Your Ambition

Now that you have Claimed Your Leadership let's move on to principle #2: Unleash Your Ambition.

Here's where I have to share my favorite poem with all of you. My favorite poem is Our Deepest Fear by Marianne Williamson, written in her book Return to Love. I think it bears sharing in this chapter. In this poem she describes completely, my thoughts and feelings on this next principle. I hope it resonates with you, the way it does with me. It always reminds me of my power within and my duty to share it with the world. I've italicized for emphasis the words that I think are really important for this principle. Although there are religious references in this poem, please feel free to substitute the word God for your own belief system, if you desire. Again, take what you like, and leave the rest.

Our Deepest Fear by Marianne Williamson

Our deepest fear is not that we are inadequate.
Our deepest fear is that we are powerful beyond measure.
It is our light, not our darkness
That most frightens us.

We ask ourselves
Who am I to be brilliant, gorgeous, talented, fabulous?
Actually, who are you *not* to be?
You are a child of God.

Your playing small
Does not serve the world.
There's nothing enlightened about shrinking
So that other people won't feel insecure around you.

We are all meant to shine,
As children do.
We were born to make manifest
The glory of God that is within us.

It's not just in some of us;
It's in everyone.

And as we let our own light shine,
We unconsciously give other people permission to do the same.
As we're liberated from our own fear,
Our presence automatically liberates others.

Are You Ambitious?

Let's just start off with a simple question. Are you ambitious? Now, I expect many of you are saying, "of course I am. Why else would I be reading this book?" However, not everyone, especially women, identifies as being ambitious even if they have an interest in leadership. ...and some of you reading this have been playing small for so long that you have forgotten about your own ambitions. You have put them on the back burner while raising kids, supporting your spouse's careers, or just telling yourself all the reasons why you can't go after that big dream that you have hidden in the recesses of your brain, perhaps still lingering from childhood or sparked by something you've just learned or seen. Still, you tell yourself, it's not for you, it's for other people.

How do you know if you're ambitious? Yes, you look outside yourself at awards you've won, goals you've achieved, and the accomplishments you have made. But if you are the woman who has been playing small, you might not have those, and it still does not mean that you are not ambitious. Even if you don't have all of those accomplishments, you can still be ambitious. It might be that ambition shows up in your life in different ways, like in how you care for your home or your children or your garden. Shift your thinking for a moment, and consider all the ways you personally demonstrate ambition in your life. Let go of the stereotypes of what ambition looks like and take a moment now for our first action step towards unleashing your ambition.

Action Step #1

Read these instructions all the way through before you begin.

Sit down with a pen and paper. If you haven't already gotten a notebook or journal for these exercises, you're going to want to do so. Now, close your eyes, and take a deep breath. Do this three times. Relax into your body and think about all the places in your life where excellence matters to you. Let your thoughts move through the different components of your life: work, home, family, how you look, how you feel, what you do in the community, your finances. Just let your mind wander through the nooks and crannies of your life and think about where it is important to you to show up as the best version of yourself or to make a difference or an impact. When you feel complete, open your eyes, and begin to journal. Allow the words to flow for as long as it takes.

This is the first evidence for your ambition, what it looks like in your own unique way, and where it shows up. I believe that we all have ambition. I don't believe that any human is innately lazy. Things can happen to create laziness, but I don't believe it to be our true nature. The more you understand about your own ambition, the more successful, impactful, and wise you will be.

If we are all ambitious creatures by nature, why aren't we unleashing it?

Why Aren't You Unleashing Your Ambition?

Let's start addressing this question by talking about cultural messages about gender and ambition.

How Culture Plays a Role

Women receive mixed messages about their ambition. On the one hand, from an early age, we are told to be good girls, to please others, and to do what is expected of us; which often means getting good grades and excelling at things like Girl Scouts, student council, ballet, and maybe even sports.

But along the way, we are also given messages that we should not overshadow our male counterparts, especially the ones we want to like us, love us, respect us, or be impressed by us. We are supposed to do well, but not "too well," especially when competing against men.

Sometimes, this occurs in overt messages, but more often, it's much more subtle than that. It's demonstrated by who our teachers pick to be leaders of groups, and captains of our teams or who our peers vote for to be President of the student council or, later, how we should consider our husband's (or partner's) feelings if we make more money than him or have a more prestigious title.

It shows up when girls start pretending to be bad at math and science or stifle their grades so as not to outshine the boy she likes or be perceived by others as "too smart."

At a young age, it's acceptable for girls to excel, but as they get older, subtle, and not so subtle messages are conveyed that it's okay to excel, but "leave the leadership, and the 'tough stuff' to the boys." We begin to inflict our own gender stereotypes. ...and although we have come a long way, these stereotypes still exist, and frankly will for many years to come. Evolution is a slow process, and cultural evolution is no exception.

Although we start out telling our children they can be anything they want to be, as they get older, we start to change our tune, and focus on being "realistic," often limiting our own and others' potential. Women are often asked to tone down their ambition. While men still tend to be encouraged (perhaps even more so as they get older) to take on positions of prestige and leadership. In contrast, when women express high ambitions, they can be told they are "too much, too bossy, too difficult, too loud…" While a man is "a go-getter, assertive, commanding, and forthright."

In addition, women still receive messages that they can't have an influential career and have children. Even today in almost 2020, there is still hot debate, politically and socially, about working vs. stay at home moms. Despite the majority of women in America working, at least part-time, outside of the home (57%) they still receive messages that they: can't be both maternal and ambitious; can't have a successful high-level career and be a good mother; that they have to choose between the two. Think about how career women are depicted in the media, often as cold, childless, and calculating. …and if you are the woman who does try "to have it both ways" she often ends up bending over backward trying to prove to herself and others that she can do it all, be everything to everyone, and not drop the ball. Can you relate?

(I actually believe you can have it all: powerful career, amazing home life, and close connection with family. But we have to change the way we view having it all; and find the balance. But that is for another book).

Those are some of the cultural and social reasons that women play small, but they certainly are not the only reasons, or no woman would be unleashing their ambition. Certainly, we have many shining examples of what unleashing our ambition looks like. We can look to women throughout history who have found a way: Ruth Bader Ginsberg, Michelle Obama, Harriet Tubman, to name just a few. So, what else is keeping you from unleashing your ambition?

You may not like the answer, but it's YOU!

That's right. It's you. You, and that thing between your ears. It's the thoughts that you have that you "can't," you're not "worthy," you're not "good enough." The thoughts that Marianne Williamson catches so beautifully in her poem above; "who am I to be brilliant, gorgeous, talented, fabulous?" and, of course, the answer is, "who are you not to be?"

<u>How Your Thinking Plays a Role</u>

In cognitive psychology, we understand the power of our thinking. Cognitive psychology believes that all of our emotions and behavior are first initiated within our thinking. We have a thought. It makes us feel a certain way, and then we act (or don't) upon that thought.

If you are flooded with positive thoughts about your potential, what you are capable of, and what you want to accomplish, you are likely to feel good and take action towards those goals. If you are flooded with negative thoughts about your abilities or likelihood for success, you will likely feel bad and unmotivated about your goals and are less likely to take the kinds of action steps that will move you forward. If your thoughts are negative enough, you may not even try.

In positive psychology, we have also talked about this in terms of a 'growth' versus a 'fixed' mindset. This comes from the work of Carol Dweck. Someone who has a growth mindset believes that things can change, you can improve, and essentially, you can grow. Just because you haven't done something yet, doesn't mean that you will not or that you cannot. The opposite is a fixed mindset. A fixed mindset sees things as unchanging, stuck, or fixed. It's the belief that if you can't do it today, you will not and cannot tomorrow. When kids are learning to tie their shoes, and they yell that they can't, and run away. They are demonstrating a fixed mindset. They can't see their possibilities in that moment (the thought, I can't). They then become flooded with anger, sadness, or disappointment (the emotion), and leave (the behavior). In many schools, they are teaching kids now to add the word yet to the end of that sentence. "I can't, yet," which demonstrates the growth mindset. I can't do it now, but there is the _possibility_ that I can, and I have the _expectation_ that I will.

Can you see now how your thoughts can hijack your ambition, even if it is there inside of you?

Action Step #2

Read these instructions all the way through before you begin.

Sit down with a paper and pen, and write this question at the top of your page: What would you do if you believed you could? If you let all of your limiting beliefs go, and there were no limits?

Now, clear your mind, set a timer for 15 minutes, and start writing as quickly as you can. Don't screen yourself. Don't let your mind give you excuses or reasons. Write anything that comes to mind as quickly as you can, even if it doesn't make any sense. We want you to tap into your deepest desires without having your rational, analytic, or socially influenced brain get in the way. If you get stuck, switch questions.* Keep writing until the timer goes off or you run out of ideas, whichever comes last. Read through if you like, but don't do anything with it yet. Put it away for now.

Here's more evidence for your ambitious nature, right here! When you get your brain out of the way, see what you can achieve.

*Some people pose this question as what would you do if you knew you could not fail? Or what would you do if you knew you would succeed? Or what would you do if you had all the resources you needed (including money) to do it? Use whichever question helps your ideas flow the most.

<u>*How Your Emotions Play a Role*</u>

Even though cognitive psychology says it is the thought that comes first, not all theories agree. I personally think that the relationship between your thinking and your emotions is bidirectional, not unidirectional. Your thinking impacts your emotions, and your emotions impact your thinking. For example, have you ever had feelings that you just didn't understand where they were coming from, and could not trace them back to a particular thought? Or have you ever woken up feeling a certain way before your brain is even online yet? That's because your emotions can be triggered by your senses: smells, sights, sounds, touch. We see this in its most extreme form in persons with trauma. People who have experienced trauma often show strong emotional reactions triggered by even subtle environmental experiences that have been perceived by their senses, even before the brain has fully registered them as a thought.

In your own life, it may look something more like playing a piece of music and having a deep emotional reaction that has nothing to do with what is going on around you. Or walking into a room, and smelling something cooking, and instantly feeling a certain way.

While your thinking is definitely critical and will need to be addressed if you want to become a Wise Leader, your emotions are also very powerful, and their influence should not be under-estimated. Both thought and emotional management are going to be essential to unleashing your ambition and becoming a Wise Leader.

The reason emotions can be so powerful is that when we have an emotion, it floods our bodies with hormones and other neurochemicals that cause physical reactions in our bodies that then either initiate or inhibit action. The stronger the emotion, the greater the physical and neurochemical response. Once these chemicals are triggered, it can take twenty minutes for your body to reset. ...and sometimes, we have no idea what or even if there was a thought that triggered it.

The emotion that most often inhibits us from unleashing our ambition is fear: fear of failure, fear of being embarrassed, fear of being visible or vulnerable, even fears about getting what we want. Fear is a powerful emotion. From an evolutionary standpoint, it is designed to keep us safe. It triggers our stress response called Fight, Flight, or Freeze. It's there for our survival. But our environments don't look like they did when our brains first evolved, so many times our more primal brain is over-reacting to its environment and keeping us more inhibited than we need to be. We don't act because we are afraid. But guess what? Have you ever heard the expression, "everything you want is on the other side of fear."

When I was studying Positive Psychology with Harvard professor, Dr. Tal Ben Shahar, he described this as "throwing your backpack over the wall." You get over your fear by going after what you want. Once you throw your backpack over the wall, there's no turning back. You're all in, and you just have to 'go for it.' That is what it takes to unleash your ambition.

Don't let your fear get in the way and rob you of what you really want. Because as Marianne says, *"And as we let our own light shine, We unconsciously give other people permission to do the same. As we're liberated from our own fear, Our presence automatically liberates others."* It's not just for you, but for everyone else whose life you are also meant to touch. ...and that is what it means to be a Wise Leader.

Why it's good news that you are a part of the problem

It's easy to blame others, the world, our culture, our society for where we are at in our life. ...and yes, I have already shown you that those things play a role. But they are not the whole story. It can be hard to look at ourselves and own our part. But you know what else it is? Liberating. Once we take ownership, there is something we can do about it. If it's always someone else's fault, then we become trapped in Learned Helplessness. We end up believing that everything is out of our control and that there is nothing we can do to change our situation. We fall into a victim mentality and become angry, hopeless, and depressed. So, it's great news that it's your fault because it gives you power. At any point, you can do something differently. You can choose to intervene at any point in the process (thinking, feeling, or behaving) to get a change in your outcomes. Just imagine what your life and our world would be like if you began to unleash your ambition upon it?

Action Step #3

Be sure to let a few days pass between Action Step #2 and #3.

Choose a time when you won't be interrupted. Put your phone on silent. Get into a nice comfortable spot in your home or somewhere private. Perhaps get one of your favorite beverages, light a candle, or put on some inspiring music. Set the tone and mood for positive thoughts and feelings. Create a positive environment for yourself to prime your brain and body for this exercise. Now get out your list from Action Step #2. Review it with an open mind. Notice how each thing on your list makes you feel. Notice any thoughts that arise. If they are negative, reframe them to something positive. Do not feed your negative thoughts or feelings. Just observe what comes up, notice which ones excite you. You may wish to circle, highlight, or underline them. Notice which ones don't really interest you. Feel free to cross them off the list. Notice which ones scare you. They might also be the ones that excite you, that's okay. Take as long as you need to go through the list, and notice the thoughts and feelings associated with each item, and put them into categories. You can group them according to the thoughts or feelings they bring up. You can group them from too easy, to difficult, to just right. Use the system that works for you, but comes from your highest thoughts and emotions.

In positive psychology, we talk about stretch goals, and this is important for unleashing your ambition. If you stay in your comfort zone, you're playing too small, and you're not unleashing your ambition or being a wise leader. If you go way too far outside of your comfort zone, you're in the panic zone. You will end up flooding yourself with fear, and going into the flight, fight, or freeze response. In unleashing your ambition, you want to be in the middle, the stretch zone. You want to choose those things that are uncomfortable, scary even, but also excite you. So anything you identified as both scary and exciting would be in your stretch zone. Go ahead, and categorize your list again now with the comfort zone, stretch zone, and panic zone.

Scratch your comfort zone items off your list. You are done playing small. Put your panic zone items on your list for the future. Now focus on on your stretch zone. Reread it, and see how you feel about it. It should feel equal parts thrilling and scary. If it doesn't, then move things around until it is just right. When you have your stretch goals, you are done with this exercise. But we will come back to it in the next section.

How to Unleash Your Ambition

So, by now, you should have already identified the places in your life that your ambition already shows up. You have an understanding of the societal and individual factors that holding you back. You've brainstormed all the things you would do if you didn't have any limits, and you've identified your stretch goals. If you haven't done any part of that, then you need to go back and do that now before moving on. ...and if you have done all of that, give yourself a pat on the back. Most people pick up books, read them, and never implement them. Doing the action steps along the way is key to actually using this book to change how you show up in the world and to truly becoming a Wise Leader.

Go ahead and get out your stretch goals list if you haven't already. I want you to look at this list and choose the one goal you are most eager to get started on. The one that really excites you and demonstrates your ambition to yourself and others.

Remember, it should be at least a little bit scary, maybe even a lot. We are not living in the comfort zone anymore or hiding out. You are Claiming Your Leadership and Unleashing Your Ambition with this.

Once you have identified the one for you, I want you to make a SMART goal out of it (specific, measurable, attainable, realistic, and timely). Many of you have done SMART goals before, but if you haven't, it is essential to do this. Many people set goals that are ineffective because they are vague, unrealistic, or have no timeline. For example, someday I am going to speak on stages around the world in front of 10 million people (and you have never spoken on any stage before). I'm not trying to limit you, but I want you to have a timeline and a measurement that lets you know if you have reached your goal. Goals can be flexible. They are not here to beat ourselves up with. They are here to use as a guide and a direction.

Once you have a SMART goal, I want you to "reverse engineer" that goal. What I mean is start with the outcome, the goal achieved, and work backwards from accomplishment to where you are sitting now. What are the action steps, thoughts, and emotions that you have to commit to accomplish your goal in the timeline you have decided upon. Now, plot those action steps on a calendar, and develop a daily routine for keeping your thoughts and emotions in alignment with your success. In Part II, you will receive lots of strategies for doing this, so keep reading. But, for now, put in your calendar the time you are going to take, each day, to keep your thoughts and emotions in check.

Okay, so you've chosen your stretch goal and turned it into a SMART goal. You've reverse engineered your thoughts, feelings, and behavioral steps that will get you to that goal. You've put it in your calendar. Still with me?

So now that you have done all that, you need to unleash it. Tell people what you are working on. Let them know how ambitious you are. But, this is important, start by only telling those you know can and will support you 100%. At this stage of the game, you don't need any nay-sayers, negative Nancys, people rooting against you or trying to "protect you from being disappointed." Only tell your cheerleaders right now, and other highly ambitious people who believe in you. But own your ambition with your whole-heart, stay focused on your goal, and remind yourself everyday of what you are working on, even on the days you can't actively work on it.

For a guided visualization to help you stay on track with unleashing your ambition, go to: www.drdonnamarino/unleash

Chapter Three: Find Your Voice

One of my clients, a very well-educated woman, and CEO, said to me over lunch, "I can't win. The women I manage think I'm too bitchy, and the older Caucasian men on my board tell me I'm too soft. So, I'm just going to do it my way."

Does that sum it up or what?

Women are constantly getting messages that they are either not strong enough, too weak, or too submissive, or, conversely, they are told they are too aggressive, abrasive, cold, or domineering. There's some truth to the statement, "I can't win." You are never going to please everyone, so stop trying. There, I said it.

Your mission as a Wise Leader is not to please everyone. It's not even to try to please everyone. It is to find your unique, authentic, and most effective way of communicating what you want and need, while also motivating and inspiring others to enroll in your mission and to be the best versions of themselves.

I know, I know, that sounds like a lot! I made it sound complicated, didn't I? Well, it doesn't have to be. In fact, usually, we make it more complicated than it needs to be. Because most of the time, when we speak from our heart, we get it right. The problem occurs when we start imitating another's way of doing things, saying things we think others want to hear or speaking from our ego, and defenses instead of what is really going on underneath. When we use our authentic voice and speak from the heart of what drives us, the right people will be drawn to your passion and will be inspired. The wrong people will be turned off. ...and that's okay! They are not your people. Bless, and release.

That is Wise Leadership, but you have to find your voice to do it. So how do you do that? Well, first, let's look at what's getting in the way. Then we'll talk about what to do about it.

<u>*What Gets in the Way of Finding Your Voice?*</u>

I've already hinted at several above, such as:

- Stereotypes and Cultural Influences
    - Cultural beliefs about how men and women communicate or *should* communicate.
    - Cultural expectations and norms of what is, and isn't *"ladylike" or masculine.*
- Imitation

- People-pleasing
- Conflict Avoidance

Stereotypes and Cultural Influences

Yes, I am going to talk about culture and stereotypes again, because frankly it's important. Now this is not to get ourselves off the hook. We still have to do our part. We can't sit in a victim mentality and blame it on society. It is for us to acknowledge what we are dealing with and come up with a strategy to deal with it. If we want society to change, we have to do our part. But we also have to acknowledge the truth of what is going on.

We have centuries of cultural consciousness regarding these ideas that, even though our beliefs have evolved and continue to evolve, they are still evident in our language, our media, our emotional reactions, and our behavior. These ideas live in our subconscious even if consciously we have rejected them. ...and this doesn't happen for just men or women, it's both.

We have certain commonly held beliefs about what it means to be masculine or feminine, and these can work both for or against us, depending upon the situation. Women, admit it, sometimes we like having things done for us. ...like the lawn mowed or a door opened for us or the drainpipe cleared. I know there are a few of you saying you like to do that yourself. Good for you if that's you, but many of us are fine with letter someone else, usually a man, do that for us. That is an example of how it can work for us. If we want more equality, we have to acknowledge both sides of the equation.

But in finding our voice, it can often work against us. Because in this particular area, there are two archetypes that play out in our collective consciousness: that of the good girl vs. the bitch. My apologies for the language, but it is the only truly effective way of conveying it, and frankly, the most often used word to describe this archetype. We are either the soft-spoken, quiet, agreeable, mild-mannered, people-pleasing, good girl archetype, or we are the out-spoken, loud, contentious, brash, abrasive, bossy, bitch archetype. One (the good girl) cannot be a leader, and the other (the bitch) is an unlikeable bulldozer.

Can you see the conundrum?

The good girl archetype aligns with cultural expectations of femininity but not leadership, and the bitch is unlikeable. So, you can be a woman or an unlikeable leader. Pretty lousy choice to have to make.

Imitation

Now let's talk about imitation. Why is this a problem? Isn't this how we often learn? Well, yes, and no. Sure, when we are just starting to learn a new skill, we often look to our role models and try to imitate them. After all, they have been successful, so why not?

Well, there are a couple of reasons why not. For one, when you are talking about high levels of leadership, such as the C-Suite (CEO, COO, CFO, et…) how many women are at the top. At the time of this writing, less than 5% of the C-Suite of Fortune 500 companies are women. So, what are the odds that if you are imitating those that have gone before you while you learn your new role that you are imitating a woman? Right? …and if you are imitating a man, is that your voice? …and how will it be received? A man and a woman can say the exact same words, and a man will be seen as assertive, in charge, effective while a woman will be seen as bossy, controlling, and domineering. So, how is that going to work out for the woman in this role?

Besides how her imitation will be received, will the woman still feel feminine in her role? Will she still feel like herself? Which brings us to the next problem with imitation; it lacks authenticity. If you are just imitating someone else, you are not bringing the full expression of yourself to the table, and everyone loses out. We need diversity and authenticity in leadership. Why? When we have a diversity of thinking, ideas, and perspective, we have more inclusion both at work and for our customers/clients. In addition, you end up with more innovation, creativity, and a higher level of product or service. Innovation and excellence come from challenging traditional schools of thought. Therefore, the more diversity at the leadership table, the better the quality of the product, whether it's a thought, an invention, an idea, what have you. If you are merely imitating, then we have agreement, but we also have more of the same. That is not Wise Leadership. That is not what will keep your company or yourself on top.

So what about authenticity. Brene' Brown has done a wonderful job of bringing authenticity into the workplace. Authentic leaders earn more trust with their employees. Trust also breeds loyalty, which leads to higher levels of productivity, more flexibility, adaptability, and retention. Authenticity is a key feature of the Wise Leader and why finding your voice is one of the principles.

People-Pleasing

People-pleasing can be seen as an extension of the "good girl" archetype. The good girl does not rock the boat, she serves others, and puts them first. Now, serving others, and putting them first, can be a leadership quality (just see Simon Sinek's book, Leaders Eat Last.) However, when taken to extremes, as in the case of many women, it is often hurtful instead of helpful. That being said, people-pleasing, when you are trying to find your voice, is like being strangled. How can you speak up, speak from the heart, or take a side if you are always worried about making everyone happy, having them like you, and not rocking the boat?

People-pleasing sabotages not only your ability to find your own voice but also your ability to lead. It's a very unhelpful characteristic often drilled into young girls and carried out to extremes as women become wives and mothers. It is counter to women becoming strong leaders.

Don't get me wrong; there is nothing wrong with being kind, thoughtful, giving, and respectful. These are wonderful traits and can be excellent virtues of the woman leader. People-pleasing is not that. People-pleasing is trying to make everyone happy and make everyone like you. There is no room for that in Wise Leadership. …and here I will say, while this may be more common among women, I have certainly seen it in the male leaders I have worked with as well. You will never find your voice if you allow yourself to stay in people-pleasing. …and that strong hold upon you not only takes away your power but robs everyone that you are meant to influence. So, as my Italian American father would have said, "Knock it off."

Conflict-Avoidance

One can quickly see how people-pleasing then leads to conflict-avoidance. I think another reason that women tend to be more conflict-avoidant is because of the ways we handle conflict itself. When boys (or men) get into a disagreement, it usually escalates quickly and resolves just as quickly. However, women tend to simmer and stew. They avoid addressing it, let it linger, and then when it does blow up, it usually takes longer to resolve. I guess you could say it's the chicken and the egg. Do we behave this way because we are conflict-avoidant or are we conflict-avoidant because we behave this way? Either way, it is ineffective. This is one of the areas that we can learn from men. We can respond to disagreement or conflict sooner, and swifter, and move on. I'm not saying imitation here. You still have to find your own voice, your own way of doing it, but there is something to learn here. If you are more focused on avoiding conflict than in expressing what you have to say and dealing with things head-on, you are going to stifle your voice, and with it, your ability to lead.

Action Step #1

Create a quiet space for you to do some reflective writing. Look back over all the ways listed above that your voice has been stifled. Begin freewriting. Write about your experiences. Where have you experienced cultural or stereotypical beliefs that have caused you to hold back? Where do you engage in imitation, people-pleasing, or conflict avoidance that has caused you not to speak up or share your opinion? Where have you been interrupted, stifled, or help yourself back? Free write on this idea, allowing your thoughts to flow onto paper. Do not screen. Do not hold back. The quicker you can write, the better. Recall any specific incidents that have occurred that have caused you to lose your voice. Keep writing until there is nothing left. Wait a few minutes to see if anything else comes to mind. Read what you have written. Add anything that needs to be added. Now destroy it. You are leaving this behind. You are committed to finding and sharing your voice. You are committed to showing up as a Wise Leader. Congratulations!

How to Find Your Voice

Now that you have released your limitations, you are ready to find your voice. This may not be easy. This may take some time, and it's definitely going to require some work on your part. You're going to have to get really honest with yourself about who you are, what your values are, and what makes you uniquely you. This may make you feel vulnerable or uncomfortable. It's going to require you to be visible, but if you want to be a leader, you know that. Let's move right into another action step that will help you begin the process.

Action Step #3

Again, find a nice quiet place for you to do some reflecting and some writing. I suggest closing your eyes and taking a few deep breaths. Now open your eyes and reflect on the words that people use to describe you. Write them down.

Look over your list. What's missing that you want to add? Go ahead and add that. Cross off anything unhelpful or negative. Add anything that embodies who you want to be, even if you don't see yourself that way yet.

Now, on another page, write down your values. This can be what is important to you, such as strength, kindness, and love. It can also be beliefs, ideology, or causes that you value. Write down what is important to you and what you stand for.

Put that page aside for a moment, and on another page, write down what makes you uniquely you. I know this one can be hard, as we often struggle to see ourselves as unique. But just write down what comes to mind. It is okay if some of the same things come up from your other lists. Just write without screening, as much as possible.

When you are done with all three lists, I want you to look at them all side-by-side. Circle the items that overlap, repeat themselves, or are similar. Circle the ones that excite you or embody the best version of yourself. When you're done, look for the common themes, and see if you can put them together in a way to describe your voice. For example, my leadership style is kind, but firm. It encapsulates leadership, femininity, and my values. See if you can come up with two or three words that you can use as a guide to describe your leadership voice.

Want More Ways to Find Your Voice?

- Say your description of your voice from the activity above every day. Write it as an affirmation, and say it in the mirror or, better yet, move some energy around by shouting it. This will help you embody it, not just think it, but live it.

- Sing. I know this sounds silly, but some women (and men too) really have to activate their ability to speak up, speak their minds, and say what they want. Finding a variety of ways to vocalize will get you used to hearing your own voice, using your voice in different ways, and activating the energy around your voice. Try it, even if it is only in the shower.

- Practice speaking up in places you would typically sit quietly, whether that is in a meeting or a social gathering. Let yourself be heard.

- Address areas of disagreement or conflict early on. Do not let them fester. Create a strategy that works for your voice of how you want to approach these situations, do it quickly and kindly.
- Practice every day, embodying your leadership voice. Find ways every day to stretch yourself and get out of your comfort zone.

- Visualize yourself using your leadership voice every morning before you get out of bed.
  For a guided visualization, go to www.drdonnamarino/unleash

- Still having trouble finding your voice? Go to www.drdonnamarino/unleash for a guided meditation to help you remove the blocks standing in the way.

Chapter Four: Lift Each Other Up!

Unfortunately, when we think of female relationships, certain stereotypes tend to arise. On the one hand, we have gal pals, girl's night out, and telling each other everything. But, on the other hand, we have gossiping, "catfighting," backstabbing, and undermining one another, especially when it comes to resources such as partners and careers. In fact, there are some women who avoid being friends with other women altogether.

But here's a question for you. Who benefits from all of this infighting? I'll give you a hint, and it's not the women. In fact, famous billionaire Warren Buffett has attributed a portion of his success to only having to compete with 50% of the population. Imagine if women were fairly represented in the competition. When we fight one another, we bring all of us down. We all lose.

In contrast, when women work together, collaborate instead of competing, and lift each other up, all women win. The rising tide lifts all boats, right? If women want to rise up in leadership, they have to work together, not against each other. They have to mentor one another, cheer each other on, and support each other. They can't default to gossip, undermining, and looking out for number one. If we want men to the gates of leadership, wealth, and opportunity, then we have to be willing to do it for each other first. Our infighting only makes it easier for those gates to remain closed.

Women currently make up 49.6% of the world's population, but in 2019, women held only 29% of senior management positions. While this was a record high, can you imagine if we held 49.6%? Or how about as world leaders. In 2019, we had 14 women leading countries in the world; Fourteen total, not a percentage. That is only 7.18% of the world's nations. What if that were 49.6%? What kind of world would we live in? What would that mean for our sons and daughters? Just ponder that for a moment.

So why do we allow ourselves to fall into the traps of holding ourselves and others down versus lifting each other up?

<u>Why Aren't We Lifting Each Other Up?</u>

Let's start with lack. Again, we have to look at evolution first. As historically, there have been more women than men in the world (51%), and we are biologically designed to keep the species going. This lack mentality initially began as a competition over resources, essentially. We first competed over mates.

Although this can still be the case, it has also infiltrated into many other aspects of our lives, including friendships, careers, money, and status. ...and because so few women are in upper-level leadership positions, this continues to perpetuate this idea of lack. There isn't enough for all. If she gets a promotion, I can't. If she does well, she's taking something away from me. These are the thoughts running through the brain of the woman with a lack of perspective.

It's a vicious circle. We instinctively compete for resources, and then we look around ourselves and only see a few women in positions of power. So, we think power and upper-level positions are scarce; therefore, we have to compete with other women instead of helping them. Therefore, continuing to enforce the idea that there isn't enough, and round, and round we go.

Here's the thing about a lack mindset. It makes you act stupid. Yeah, I said it. The lack mindset makes you act stupid. You get competitive, sneaky, backstabbing, and jealous. Nothing good comes of believing that you don't have enough, or there isn't enough to go around or that when someone else wins, you lose, especially when it comes to your fellow woman. It just becomes a contributor in keeping us small. While this may have originated to preserve the species, it obviously does not serve us now, and it's time to let it go. We'll talk about how to let it go in just a bit, but as we have discussed in the earlier chapters, remember the brain is slow to adapt UNLESS you _consciously_ choose to think and act differently.

So, a lack mindset is one reason we don't lift each other up, but then we have to look at who benefits when women in-fight. Here's the thing, I'm not saying men are bad. I want to be very clear about that. I am just saying that in any situation where someone is an "underdog," treated unfairly, or kept out of something, we have to look at the why and at who benefits from it.

Who stands to gain?

When we in-fight, we give our power away. Please let that sink in for a minute. When we fight with one another, we give away our power to everyone else. If you are giving away your power, there will always be someone there ready to take it. If we are too busy fighting one another, we miss out on more important things like banding together to take back our power. We miss out on our full potential. We get distracted from the important things.

Our in-fighting allows others to take advantage of our distracted state. In the end, it helps to support the patriarchy, rather than challenge it. Now, again, I'm not saying men should not have power. I'm just saying we should have our fair share, and that when we do, we will ALL benefit from it. Diversity of ideas at the leadership table will help us include others, see new perspectives, and develop new ideas. We will be more inventive, innovative, visionary, and creative. It's truly a win-win.

But for those calling the shots, it can be scary to share, at least for some. They too have a lack mindset. So, when we fight, we do the work for them. The work of keeping us out, and we leave the leadership to them. You can see their lack mentality rise when you hear fear and judgement when women are promoted to positions of power, whether in a government office, the board room, or in their communities.

Fear and judgement are key signs of a lack mentality. Men who fear women coming into power are acting from a belief that women are taking something away from them. They are acting from scarcity and contraction rather than abundance and expansion. Rather than seeing what they are gaining from a balance in leadership, they are focused on the thought of losing. Both genders have to shift this perspective. Imagine living in a world where we believed that there was enough to go around. That one person's success did not take away from your's but actually amplified each other's. How would we think, act, and treat one another differently? The Wise Leader believes in enough for all and isn't afraid to lift each other up.

This is why men and women have to do their part in shifting this dynamic and creating gender parity. It's not just a one-or-the-other job. We both have a part to play.

<u>*How Do We Lift Each Other Up?*</u>

It starts by choosing to consciously move from a mindset of lack to one of abundance. Bear with me here, but there is actually no reason to believe in lack. I know this is a tough one. I know you are saying, "but Dr. Donna, I can see lack all around me." The truth is, you're not wrong. Sure you can find evidence for lack, but how does it benefit you? Has feeling like you don't have enough, never will have enough, or are incapable of ever getting enough, ever made anything good happen for you? Has your feeling of lack or scarcity ever made you act better towards others? I ask you this, what purpose does it serve? If it's not helping you, then make another choice.

You will always find evidence of whatever you look for. It's called confirmation bias. It's part of why gratitude practices are so effective in treating depression. When you look for things to feel grateful for, you'll find them, and you'll feel better. If you choose to believe in abundance, if you choose to look for all of the evidence in your life for abundance, and focus on that, you will find evidence for that instead. You get to choose. What you focus your attention on grows. If you want more lack, focus on that. But if you want abundance, focus on abundance. If you want a promotion or leadership position focus on, and celebrate whenever a friend or colleague, especially a woman, gets one. She's not taking it away FROM you. She's paving the way FOR you.

Here's the thing about choosing to believe in abundance, when you consciously choose to believe that there is enough for everyone, you empower yourself and others. You suddenly have a chance to have anything you desire, and because you have a chance, so do others. It becomes okay to help others because you don't have to compete. If there is enough for all, it actually becomes easy to lift each other up. There's really no advantage not to! Instead, there becomes safety in numbers. Every win for one woman is a win for another, instead of a threat. It completely shifts the energy from moving against, to moving towards, from contraction to expansion. When women band together and support each other, they can help one another rise up into leadership. As they rise up, they also pave the way for others.

Shifting your mindset from lack to abundance is first a decision, and then a practice. First, you have to fully commit to changing your mindset. Then you have to back it up with action. You have to practice believing in abundance, noticing it around you, and acting as if. When you catch yourself believing or acting from lack, you have to snap out of it and shift. <u>You need to retrain your brain</u>. The saying goes, neurons that "fire together wire together." If you want to change your thinking, you need repetition. That repetition is what changes your brain to create new automatic thoughts, and then the action helps you embody it.

From this abundance mindset, you can then take conscious action to lift your fellow women up. What would that look like? It could be throwing a party for another woman who was just promoted. It could be creating a mastermind of like-minded women to help brainstorm ideas on how to advance their careers or businesses. It could be supporting a woman running for office or offering to lend a hand to a woman just starting out in her career or business. Whatever action you take, it's showing a woman that I've got your back. We are in this together. I support you.

Think of it this way: Change the thought, change the action, get the result. Choose to embody being the woman who lifts others up. Many of you have probably seen this quote floating around social media: Be the woman who fixes another woman's crown without telling the world that it was crooked."

And if you are a man reading this book, I would recommend the same actions. Replace your lack mindset with abundance, and support your female coworkers, colleagues, family members, and friends in being successful. Celebrate their wins, and help pave the way, not based on gender, but based on merit. If you are a leader, man or woman, be a mentor.

For guided visualizations to break through your lack mindset, consciously choose abundance, and take tangible action to lift each other up, go to www.drdonnamarino.com/unleash

Chapter Five: The Power of Purpose

Now, I'm certainly not the first person to talk about purpose. Most of you have probably heard of Simon Sinek and his books on the topic, It Starts with Why, and Know Your Why, to name a few of the books out there. But here we are going to discuss it here as the Fifth principle in Wise Leadership. This principle is the fuel for your fire. It encompasses your why as a leader, but also your life's purpose, what you feel called to do. For some you, these two things might be the same, but for others, they may not. Sometimes our why is inspired by our life events while our life's purpose is 'a knowing' that we have. The two are intermingled, but not always the same. The important part is for you to identify each and to make them as powerful as possible.

Why? Because the more powerful your purpose, your why, the easier it will be for you to stay focused, persistent, and consistent in your efforts. If your purpose is weak, you won't make it. If it just for money or prestige, for example, it is not likely going to be enough to sustain you over the long haul. Your why has to be deeply meaningful, in order to keep forging forward. In the case of money or prestige, think about why you really want those things. Perhaps, it is to provide for your family, to start a charity or to contribute to an organization, to use your influence for good. Those are the real reasons, and the ones that will take you farther.

To be a leader, you have to be strong. You have to be driven. Ambitious. The road will get hard. There will be challenges. If your purpose isn't strong enough, if you don't know your why, you will lose direction and give up. Period. End of Story.

As a leader, your job is also to enroll others in your mission. Leading is not a solitary job. It's the head of a team. You're not just leading yourself, right? Leaders lead, and guide others. They show you the way. They share their vision and get people excited about it. A good leader inspires their team with their vision and makes them want to be a part of it. The more people you want to impact, the more powerful your purpose/why needs to be.

If you do not have a powerful purpose, who is going to want to follow you? Who is going to get on your bandwagon and help you fulfill your vision? No one. The power of purpose inspires others. It creates loyalty, community, collaboration, persistence, and resilience. Without it, you and your team are likely to get bored, restless, disinterested, and eventually will look for something else more satisfying. They will abandon ship.

For example, in the introduction, you read about my personal purpose. Now, if you are still reading this book, that purpose spoke to you. You were perhaps moved by my story, my motivation, and my goals. If you weren't, then you probably aren't reading this now, so I won't keep talking to you. But, you see how that works... ...those of you who stuck around.

And knowing my personal purpose, you can see how it is powerful and motivating not just for those that I enroll in my mission, but for myself too. When it gets hard, when I hit a roadblock, when someone doesn't finish reading my book...I can draw from my why. I can think about my father, my sister, and all the people that I know I am meant to help, inspire, and lift up, and guide, and I can manage through the rough patches to keep ongoing. No matter what. A lesser why may not be enough fuel for such a big vision. This is one case where size does matter. The bigger, the better.

Let's shift a little to talk more specifically about life purpose as it relates to Wise Leadership and the Power of Purpose. Again, this might be one and the same as your why, but it may not be. For example, my life purpose is to change other's lives by creating more conscious (wise) leaders, and bringing more diversity to the leadership table, so that we improve quality of life for all on a global scale. But my why stems from my losses. My why informs my purpose, but they are not exactly the same. They are related but not the same. Both are a part of my motivation; both enroll others in my mission; both keep me going.

I truly believe that our role here on earth is to contribute, whether you embrace being a wise leader or not. I believe that we all have a contribution to make using our own uniqueness. We all have a unique set of gifts, talents, abilities, passions, and strengths. The place where these all come together is connected to our purpose or our particular way of contributing. We need only look at ourselves and our life stories to figure it out. It's not the mystery that some believe. The answers lie in who you naturally are and what your life experience has taught you.

Your purpose should excite you. It should burn in your belly. It should light you up and make you want to contribute. It doesn't have to mean changing the world, although it could. Each person's purpose is different, and it only needs to have importance and gravitas to themselves and the people that they are meant to impact. If you don't feel passionate about it, then it's not your purpose. If you do, that passion will inspire others and enroll them in your mission.

Strategies for Igniting your Power of Purpose

- Write about your Why

- Write your Mission Statement

- If you are unclear on your purpose, draw a Venn Diagram. Write your passions in one circle, your strengths in the other, and the places/activities/jobs etc... where these things come together in the middle where the circles overlap. This will give you a great guide to your purpose and what you should be doing in life. *For a downloadable worksheet to complete this exercise go to* www.drdonnamarino.com/unleash

- If you are still unclear (or you want clarity on any question) download the Future Self guided visualizations at www.drdonnamarino.com/unleash

- Read your Why, and your Mission Statement every day
- Begin sharing your Purpose with others, expand your circle of who knows

- Put up pictures, images or words in your workspace to remind you of your Why/Purpose when times get tough

Part II: Overcoming the Obstacles to Your Success

Introduction

Now that you have learned the principles of Wise Leadership let's take a look at some of the most common obstacles to putting them into place in the real world. When we make changes to ourselves to stand more boldly in our leadership and our truth, it is not uncommon for obstacles such as fear, imposter syndrome or even time to pop up and try to derail us from our newfound commitment to ourselves and others. In this section of Unleashing the Wise Leader, we will explore the most common obstacles and what to do about them as they arise so that your Wise Leadership does not get derailed. Expect obstacles to happen. That is human nature. Just plan for how you will manage them.

Chapter 6: The Boogeyman (aka Fear)

The boogeyman, the thing that goes bump in the night, that shadow in the corner of your room when you were a little girl under the covers, eyes wide open... frightened. You know what I'm talking about

Now there are times that fear can actually be a gift. Like when it is based in reality, or when it is used as a guidance system to keep us out of danger, or when it is our intuition telling us that something has gone awry here... then it is a gift. That is why we have this emotion in the first place, to give us an internal system that will help keep us safe. But too much of the time, it's none of those things. It's just fear, for no **real** reason.

The problem is, as a society, we have become addicted to fear. We are in 'fear overdrive.' Just look at our news. People unconsciously or not like the adrenaline rush they get from fear, and that rush reinforces the feeling. Some of you are living in fear every day. It has become a habit of thinking, feeling, and (not) doing. Unfortunately, it is a pattern that keeps you small and from fulfilling your dreams, because with fear comes avoidance. We believe by avoiding the things that make us afraid, we won't have to feel afraid anymore. Except what we really do is train ourselves _not to even try_. If we don't try, we don't have to be scared, we can't fail, and we can avoid "the worst."

Ironically, the avoidance actually reinforces the fear, creating more of it, not less. It's simple really. What we reward, we get more of. When we avoid, we are actually rewarding our fear. We learn to believe there must be something scary over there (fear) and that only by staying away (avoidance), we stayed safe (reward), even when there is actually nothing to be afraid of.

The avoidance robs us of the lesson that disempowers our fear; that there was actually nothing to be afraid of in the first place. That is why fear IS the boogeyman. All shadows and no substance, but still keeping you scared under the covers like a little girl. But you are not a little girl anymore. You'll never be that small and helpless again. It's time you stand up to your fear and become its master.

If you are going to start to live the principles of Wise Leadership, you are going to have to. Because let me tell you something, the fear is not going to go away. In fact, I hate to say this, but it may get worse. Whenever we make a big change, a big shift, especially in who we are, our identity, the fear will spike. It will try to keep us in the status quo or what we are used to (more on status quo in chapter 10). It likes homeostasis, and it will try to get you back to your default settings.

I refer to this process of 'growing into your leadership,' and to shifting your identity as 'up-leveling.' We are up-leveling ourselves, growing, expanding, and changing. To be a leader, you have to. You have no choice. It's part of breaking away from the smaller version of yourself. This means breaking ties with your old identity, your old patterns of thinking, feeling, and behaving. You can't just stop growing. You can't just stay the same. You've heard the expression before, "If you want something you've never had before, you have to do something you've never done." Or it's counter, "If you always do what you've always done, you'll always get what you've always gotten."

If you want to claim your leadership, and you never have before, it's going to be scary, but what are you going to do about it? This is the leader's journey. Do you think other leaders don't feel fear? Absolutely not. It's not about NOT feeling fear. It's about managing it. It's about not succumbing to it. That is what real bravery is, and that is what a leader is, brave. Leaders guide; leaders think for themselves; leaders break the status quo. Leaders face their fears and do the next right thing. …and you will too.

If you want to accept your role as a Wise Leader, whether that means at home, at work or in the world, for you, you have to get comfortable with fear, learn how to manage it, learn when it is there to support you, and when it is there to keep you playing small. But you can do it. Maybe not perfectly. That's okay. Wise leadership is not about perfection. It's about progress. It's about change. It's about potential. It's about being the best version of yourself, so that others can to. It's about the world being a better place because you are in it. …and that means not letting fear bully you out of fulfilling your part of the Wise Leadership movement.

****

If you allow fear and it's lovely companion, "what if" syndrome, they will rob you of your dreams. They will sneak in during the night and collect your most precious ones if you don't learn how to keep them out.

Let me ask you this: How come we always ask what if…. (fill in most horrific outcome), and not what if….(fill in best case scenario)? Why do we think we are so much more likely to end up in the worst-case scenario than the best?

<u>Let me tell you why</u>.

Our brain is hardwired to do so. It's called the Negativity Bias, which simply means that our brains are wired to see the negative before they register the positive. Negative events (or the threat of negative events) have more salience in our brains than the positive. In fact, researchers have suggested that it takes as many as three to five positive events to have the same mental impact as one negative event. If you think of the neurons in your brain as roads and highways, it means that negative events get to ride on the superhighway cruising along at 80mph, while your positive events are stuck on a two-lane road in morning traffic.

We are wired this way, once again, due to evolution, that extremely slow process. At the time of our creation, in order for our species to survive, we had to be alert of any potential threats. Those who were really good at that survived, and those that weren't, didn't. Only, now this works at our disadvantage. For most of us we are not concerned about survival on a daily basis. There isn't something ready to pounce on us and eat us for lunch if we make a wrong turn, but our brains and our bodies are not fully convinced of this yet.

The good news is that we now know that the brain can be retrained. It is malleable. There was a time when scientists believed that our brains were fixed, but now we know that they are plastic and that with LOTS of repetition, we can put negativity in the two-lane traffic and positivity on the superhighway.

Strategies for Overcoming Fear

So, how do you do this? I'm not saying it is easy, but there are some simple action steps that you can take.

Increasing your Positivity Ratio

Remember that 3:1 rule of positive to negative events? Let's start there. This is known as your positivity ratio (Fredrickson, and Losada), and while it's math has come under scrutiny, the empirical evidence still demonstrates that higher positivity ratios are correlated with flourishing. Obviously, if one is flourishing, they are not also living in fear.

If you want to retrain your brain and stop making fear your default setting, one way is to increase your positivity ratio is by crowding out your fear with increased experiences of positivity and bravery. In doing so, you will retrain your brain to see the possibilities over the dangers. There are three ways to do this: increasing your positivity boosters, increasing your positivity enablers, and decreasing your negative influences (Fredrickson). This means doing more of things that lead to positive emotions for you, such as favorite hobbies, spending time with loved ones, savoring your experiences, practicing gratitude etc… These are the positivity boosters. The enablers are the things that lay the foundation for feeling positive, such as getting enough rest, exercise, and good nutrition. Think of it this way, if you haven't slept in 3 days, and then go do your favorite activity, how much can you enjoy it? The positivity enablers are the lifestyle choices that get you functioning at your best to lean into your positive experiences throughout the day. Finally, the negativity reducers are where you cut out or reduce the negative experiences in your life like watching fear-based news stories or television shows, letting go of unhealthy relationships or habits, not engaging in gossip, or "whoa is me" conversations.

I recommend making three lists: positivity boosters, positivity enablers, and negativity reducers. Just brainstorm as many things as you can put on each column or list. Then choose one or two items to focus on over the next 30 days, and see where your level of fear drops too, and where your level of positivity raises to. Start by ranking each on a scale from 1-10 today, and again in 30 days. This exercise can be found in the companion workbook.

Challenging your Fear-Based Thoughts

Fear-based thoughts are going to happen. As long as you are alive, you will have them, at least from time to time. But we are going to work on reducing the frequency (how often), duration (for how long), and intensity (how severe is it) of this thinking. This is not about never having fear again, but it's about not letting it bully you, and learning how to reduce the experience of it, and manage it when it crops up is key.

Let's start by doing a little assessment of where you are at. It's always good to know where you are starting from so you can celebrate all of your wins along the way. It can be easy to overlook the small wins if we aren't aware, and celebrating is how we reinforce the wins so that we have more of them. You want to build upon the energy of your successes, not your failures. What you focus your attention on grows. Focus on your failure, and you'll get more of that, focus on your success, and you will get more of that. So, let's figure out where you are, so we'll know how far you've come.

If you aren't already, go to a place where you won't be disturbed for a few minutes. Close your eyes and get comfortable in a seated or lying down position. Briefly scan your body for any tension and give your muscles permission to relax. Take a few deep breaths. Now envision yourself going through your day, a typical day, and tune into your experience as if it is already happening. Notice what your first thought is when you get out of bed, what are you thinking as you get yourself ready in the morning, how do you feel? Take yourself through the course of your day, step by step, as if it is actually happening, and tune into the thoughts and feelings that arise. Notice where and when fear creeps in. What is the thought? How intense is the feeling? What are the triggers? How often do they occur? When you have completed your day in your mind, and find yourself back in bed, slowly and gently open your eyes, take out your journal or Wise Leader Workbook, and begin to write about your experience. Rate your level of fear frequency, duration, and intensity on a scale from 1-10. This is your starting point. *

(*for an audio recording of this exercise, go to www.drdonnamarino.com/unleash)

Now that you have a baseline and know where your starting point is, we can begin to work on transforming your fear-based thoughts.

Go ahead and get out your journal or Wise Leader Workbook. If writing in your own journal, draw a line down the middle of the page. On the top of one column, write "Fear-based thoughts." On the top of the other column, write "What I could say instead." Start with the fear-based thoughts, and just brainstorm. Write down as many as you can think of that pop up on an ordinary day or when you step outside your comfort zone. When you think of being a Wise Leader, what fear-based thoughts come up? When you think of fulfilling your dreams, what fear-based thoughts come up? Write them all down WITHOUT judgement. You are just dumping them out. If you can't see them, you can't challenge them.

Once you have written them all down, I want you to reframe them. Look at each fear-based thought and write a better thought in the column next to it.

Now, when you are done with that column, go ahead, and rank each "better thought" how much you actually believe it, on a scale from 1-10. If it is not an eight or higher, rewrite it to something that is more believable for you, at least an eight or higher. If you don't believe it, it won't work. Studies show that this is the problem with affirmations. If they are so far out of your belief, you can say them until you are blue in the face, and your subconscious will reject them. You can always work your way up to what you want to believe, but you have to start where you are at. These are called ladder thoughts. They are the thoughts that are the rungs of the ladder to get you where you want to be. You can't go from the bottom of the ladder to the top without climbing the rungs.

Okay, now that you have your baseline, you have your thoughts, and your reframes, you need to practice them. Throughout the day, I want you to "catch" your thoughts, and whenever you catch yourself in fear-based thinking, I want you to say your new more positive version of that thought. It may be hard in the beginning because these thoughts have become second-nature. In fact, we call these automatic thoughts because they are so ingrained, we don't realize they are happening. One way to know you have stepped into fear-based thinking is to notice how you feel. What does your body feel like when you step into fear? If suddenly you find that uncomfortable feeling in your chest or your stomach or you suddenly feel the emotion of fear and discomfort, but you don't know why, tune in to your thinking. Ask yourself, what am I thinking about? What is the story that I am telling myself? Is that true? Do I want to believe that story? What would be a better feeling thought right now that I could believe?

In the beginning, you might have to go through this process dozens or even hundreds of times a day, depending on where you are starting from, but the more you do it, the more it will become a habit, and then your "better thinking" thoughts will become your automatic thoughts, and ride the superhighway in your brain. This is how you retrain your brain out of fear-based thinking as a habit.

Now, you might need reminders to practice this new behavior. This is where an anchor can be very handy. An anchor is a reminder to anchor in your new habits. It is something you attach meaning to that you will see frequently. This could be a rubber band or string on your wrist. I often recommend a piece of jewelry like a ring, bracelet, or necklace. It's a nice reward for committing to this new behavior, and every time you see it, you will be reminded to check your thoughts, reframe, and celebrate this new way of being. Anything that you ascribe this meaning to, and that you will see, and often notice throughout your day will work.

Visualization

Visualization will help you to embody this new way of being. It is mental rehearsal. You rehearse in your mind how you want to handle the situations that would normally bring up fear. The most important part of visualization is to use all of your senses to feel into it as if it is really happening. Our brain does not know the difference between imagination and reality. The more we mentally rehearse how we want to be in situations, the more we train our brain to actually be that way when the time comes. It's like muscle memory for your brain. Your training it how to behave in certain situations, so the more real you can make it, the more your brain will believe it and respond that way. That is why top athletes all use visualization in addition to physical training.

Take 5 minutes each day to visualize yourself embodying being a wise leader. See yourself in what you would wear, how you would move, and speak. Where are you? Who is with you? What are the sights, sounds, smells, textures, even tastes all around you? Perhaps for you, it is imagining yourself on stage or in a conference room. Perhaps it's running a PTA meeting or political event. Whatever it means to you personally to be a Wise Leader, imagine yourself claiming that role and fully embodying it in as much detail as possible. For additional help with this exercise, you can download a guided visualization at www.drdonnamarino.com/unleash.

Summary

- Real fear is a tool to keep us safe, and we should both listen and be grateful for it.

- Unfounded fear keeps us playing small and stuck in "what if" syndrome.

- Although we are wired, due to the negativity bias, to see the potential negative outcomes of something before the positive, we can change that.

- Our brains are malleable, and we can override our evolutionary tendencies with attention and repetition.

- You can overcome your fear by increasing your positivity ratio, challenging your fear-based thoughts, and visualizing yourself mastering situations in which you currently feel fear.

- With consistent practice of these exercises, you can minimize the impact of fear on your life and keep it from getting in the way of your Wise Leadership.

Chapter 7: Imposter Syndrome (Self-Worth & Self-Doubt)

Imposter Syndrome. We all have it. Even the most successful people in the world experience it. Yet, somehow, we all think that we are the only ones. People like Sheryl Sandberg, COO of Facebook, and Mike Cannon-Brooks, CEO, and successful entrepreneur, admit to feeling this way in the midst of all of their success (if you haven't seen Mike Cannon-Brooks TEDx talk on the subject, you must). So, are you surprised that you might feel it to?

What is Imposter Syndrome? It's the belief that people are going to find out that you are a fraud. That no matter how much success you have had, people will discover that it was some kind of fluke, and you aren't really who they think you are. Is this starting to sound familiar?

Well, relax, it's okay. As I said, you are not alone.

Can you see, though, how this could keep you from claiming your leadership, unleashing your ambition, or finding your voice? After all, do you want to call attention to yourself if you fear being "found out?" Probably not.

But what is Imposter Syndrome really about, underneath it all? What causes this niggling feeling that you don't belong here? The answers lie in the body and in the brain's desire for homeostasis, as well as your personal levels of self-worth, deservedness, and self-doubt.

These are often the root causes of Imposter Syndrome. The causes that must be slain if you are going to show up and do your work in the world as a Wise Leader. Now, this doesn't mean that you have a terrible case of low self-esteem if you are struggling with Imposter Syndrome. You might, but certainly even the most confident people have had a case of imposter syndrome from time to time. For most people, it has to do with both your conscious and your unconscious beliefs about who you are.

If you are experiencing Imposter Syndrome, there is most likely an insecurity lurking deep within your brilliant mind as you continue to climb the ladder of success. You, yourself, may not have adjusted to this new success as a part of your identity, which can then open the door to doubt, and insecurity. Unfortunately, no matter how successful you become, it doesn't seem to satisfy your insecurity's insatiable appetite for proof that you don't belong here. It feasts on even the faintest whispers of doubts, fears, questions, and old stories, fueling its belief that, in fact, you don't (belong).

Homeostasis

When you are stepping outside your comfort zone, taking on more leadership, and taking actions that are not in alignment with your old patterns of thinking, the old parts of you begin to shout, "Imposter!" They see you as the old you, not the new. They have not yet accommodated this new success. Therefore, they reject it. Our brains, and bodies like homeostasis, so they try to pull you back to your default settings, the you that they know and love. They reject this new version of yourself by telling you you're a fraud. You don't belong. This isn't you.

It's okay, though. It's just a part of your up-leveling into this new ideal of who you are, a part of your own expansion. The more you understand what is happening and why; the more you can dismiss it as a part of the process and not give it weight as a true statement on who you are, the more easily you will be able to defeat it. It will be an interesting thought rather than a declaration.

A way to minimize imposter syndrome is to practice seeing yourself as having incorporated this success into your identity before it has even happened. The more you see yourself as a leader, as this successful version of yourself, the less you will reject it when things start to shift outside of yourself, and others begin seeing you as a leader too. The exercises in Claiming Your Leadership will help pave the way for that. Go back, and redo them if you feel imposter syndrome creeping in, but don't forget the power of visualization (aka mental rehearsal) in preparing your brain for who you are becoming. The most important thing is to practice it regularly and to use all of your senses to immerse yourself in the feeling and the knowing of being the Wise Leader.

Self-Worth, Deservedness, and Self-Doubt

Now let's take a look at the role of self-worth, deservedness, and self-doubt.

Whereas homeostasis speaks to our biological wiring, and how it can fight us as we move into leadership; self-worth, deservedness, and self-doubt speak to our mental, emotional, and behavioral conditioning. These are not hard-wired into us like the desire for homeostasis but are learned from our environment and our experiences.

Issues of worth, deservedness, and doubt are naturally exacerbated in all marginalized populations, including but not limited to, women. The act of marginalizing a population sends conscious and subconscious messages to the people being marginalized that they are somehow less worthy, less deserving, and less capable, which is why they are less valued, underpaid, given fewer opportunities, and historically have rights/decisions taken away from them. When your history is littered with examples of this such as slavery, not being given the right to vote, or unequal pay for the same work, the seed is planted in the mind whether you consciously choose to believe them or not, that you do not have the same level of worth, and deservedness as others, and that you have reason to second-guess yourself, and doubt your abilities.

In order to live the principles of Wise Leadership, you will need to consciously choose to up-level your sense of self-worth, your intrinsic value, and your level of deservedness while also squashing your second-guessing, self-doubting, thoughts, and behaviors. Are you up for the challenge?

I know, it's simple to say, not so easy to do, but totally possible.

How? It's like peeling an onion. First, we start with the outer layers (consciousness), and then we move in towards the center (subconsciousness).

Let's begin.

Unpacking Self-Worth, and Deservedness

First, let's clarify the difference between self-worth and deservedness. They are not actually the same thing. You can feel worthy of something, but not believe you deserve it, and vice versa. In order to get where you want to be, you will need high levels of both.

Let's start with deservedness. Deservedness implies a sense of having earned something. It implies that you have done something that is deserving of a particular outcome. For example, "I deserve this because… I am a good person. I am educated. I have worked hard. Someone owes me…." You can see the many reasons someone may consciously or unconsciously come to the conclusion that they deserve something. You can see the many ways we can rationalize how we have earned something, and that it should now be ours for the taking. This may be true or untrue, but your belief in your own deservedness is going to allow you or disallow you to have things and to believe in yourself. If you feel you do not deserve that promotion, you are more likely to struggle with Imposter Syndrome than if you believed that you do.

Now, some people really struggle with deservedness because they equate it to entitlement. Deservedness at its extreme, when it comes from ego and arrogance, can certainly move into entitlement, but that is not what we are talking about here. We are talking about a healthy level of deservedness that acknowledges your gifts, talents, efforts, and intentions. It is a healthy sense of confidence and self-awareness that feels very different than entitlement. Ironically, I have never met a truly entitled person who worried about this; so, if you are afraid that your deservedness is entitlement, you can rest assured that it is not. The entitled never question their deservedness. Feel free to boost your deservedness without fear.

Worthiness, on the other hand, suggests more of an innate value. It is less about doing and earning than about being and receiving. It is more about saying, "I value myself enough to know that I should receive this good fortune/success," etc... Often times, it is easier to point to our accomplishments and say that we "deserve" something than it is to say that we have some type of intrinsic value that makes us worthy. But the truth is that you do and learning to accept that is an important part of taking your place as a Wise Leader.

I have had many high-achieving, hard-working clients who have struggled with this idea that their mere existence is enough to prove their worth. I challenge you to believe this. So many of us have been trained that we are only worthy because of our accomplishments. I am going to suggest that if your heart is calling for you to stand up as a Wise Leader, you are already worthy. You would not have been given this yearning if you were not meant to fulfill it. If you are meant to fulfill it, then you must be worthy of doing so. It may take some time for you to accept this, but I believe it is worth working on in order to make your mark in the world.

Practical Strategies for Increasing Self-Worth, and Deservedness

Here are some helpful strategies for improving your feelings and beliefs of worthiness, and deservedness:

- First, make the conscious decision that you are going to increase your level of worthiness and deservedness. Renew this choice each day. Say it out loud, "I choose to intentionally, and consciously increase my feelings of self-worth, and deservedness."

- Second, create a worthiness/deservedness affirmation, and say it to yourself every morning upon rising. Begin your affirmation with the words I am. This registers a sense of ownership and embodiment in the mind. Examples are: I am worthy and deserving of leadership. I am worthy and deserving of making a difference in the world. I am worthy and deserving of sharing my ideas with others. I am worthy and deserving of standing up for what I believe in. Say it out loud while looking in the mirror at least once a day.

- Third, create a worthiness/deservedness ritual for the morning. It could be writing your affirmation down ten times or a list of all the reasons you are worthy and deserving. It could be creating a nice breakfast for yourself and savoring it. It could be reading inspiring quotes from others, using luxurious soap in the shower, or something else that makes you feel decadent, luxurious, or pampered.

- Finally, to really tap into subconscious beliefs about self-worth, and deservedness use hypnosis, EFT (emotional freedom technique), or guided meditations to help rewire your brain around these belief systems. You can find a hypnosis track here at www.drdonnamarino.com/unleash

Self-Doubt, and Imposter Syndrome

Increasing our sense of worth and deservedness may help to decrease our self-doubt. However, it is still possible to believe in our worth and deservedness but to doubt our decision making, our purpose, or even our abilities and opportunities. We may get that promotion but then feel like an imposter because we doubt our ability to meet up to our own expectations in the role (or others) despite feeling that we were worthy or deserving of the role. You may experience these feelings if you are new to leadership and stepping into this role for the first time. You may believe that you deserved the chance and that you were as good a candidate as any, but then when you get the opportunity, fear and self-doubt can creep in, leading to thoughts of being a fraud or an imposter.

Curbing your self-doubt is an important part of being a Wise Leader and embracing the principles of Wise Leadership.

Culturally speaking, it seems that women are taught to doubt themselves and second guess their decisions more than men. They may even be more prone to Imposter Syndrome. Research shows that women are less likely to apply for promotions and ask for raises. ...and when they do (ask for raises), they don't ask for as much as a man will. In addition, they are more likely to attribute their promotions and career success to luck or being in the right place at the right time. This has been found even among some of the most successful women in the world, and across professions.

If we want to step into Wise Leadership, we have to be willing to let go of self-doubt, to stand up assured in our abilities, and in our decision making. We have to see ourselves as equals. We CAN be feminine and competent and confident.

Strategies for Tackling Self-Doubt

Practice these strategies to overthrow your self-doubt, and step into your Wise Leader:

- The first step (again) is in consciously choosing to no longer allow yourself to live in self-doubt. Write it, read it, say it out loud. Make the conscious choice every day to let it go. Decide that you are no longer going to doubt yourself; your abilities, your decisions, your desires, none of it.

- Create an affirmation. I have a t-shirt that I especially love that says, Breath in Confidence, Exhale Doubt." Perhaps something like that will work for too. If so, take a moment (or two or three…) each day to stop and breathe and say this to yourself. Remember, "I am" statements are the most powerful affirmations. A statement like, "I am a confident decision-maker" may be the trick for you. The important thing is that it resonates with you; that you can feel it in your gut or your heart as being true for you.

- When you find yourself with doubting thoughts, observe them, detach from them, and send them on their way. This is a practice. You are building new confidence muscles and letting your self-doubt muscles whither. Be kind and compassionate with yourself, but don't allow them to take up space in your head. Witness the self-doubt, and let it float on by, like a cloud in the sky.

- Create a list of all of the reasons that you can trust yourself. The opposite of doubt is trust. Show yourself the evidence that you are trustworthy.

- For an audio track by Dr. Donna to boost your confidence, and let go of self-doubt, go to www.drdonnamarino/unleash

Summary

- Imposter syndrome (feeling like a fraud), although common among successful people, can stall you in your tracks if you let it.

- To become a Wise Leader, you are going to have to conquer this foe.

- At the root of Imposter Syndrome lies the brain and body's desire for homeostasis or the status quo, as well as feelings of low self-worth and deservedness combined with elevated self-doubt.

- This combination can prevent you from accomplishing your leadership goals. However, there are several strategies that can help you overcome these obstacles.

- With a regular practice of affirmations, visualization, and conscious decision making, you can prepare your brain, and body for your new Wise Leader identity while increasing your worth, and deservedness, and decreasing self-doubt.

- It all starts with awareness, and conscious decision making to increase your worth, and deservedness while decreasing your self-doubt.

Chapter 8: Time & Money (Scarcity Mindset)

Probably the two biggest excuses I hear from almost everyone that I meet on why they don't take action on something they want are time and money. Guess what? These really are just excuses. Let me give you an example. My mom used to say, "Want to get something done? Ask a busy person." What did she mean by this? Those that should have the time excuse don't because they are too busy accomplishing. Other people are getting done the very things that you say you want. How can they do it, and you can't? They may have more money than you, that's true, but we all have the same amount of time. If they can do it, you can too. It's all about choices and priorities.

Here's the problem with using time and money as an excuse. The problem is that when you complain of not having the time or money to do something that is important to you, you are standing in a place of lack, a place of resistance, and a place of missed opportunity. You end up blocking the solution from coming to you.

You may not have as much time or money as you would like, but when you really want something, you will find a way, if you are open. Perhaps, you have to start small, or you may choose to ask for help. When you tell yourself that there is a way, even when you cannot see it, the way will often appear. When you just fold your arms and say there is no time or money, then you are right. You are stuck, and you lose. There is no moving forward.

It puts you into a place of scarcity and blocks the way from revealing itself. Often, we do this because, on a subconscious level, we are actually afraid of moving forward. There is something else going on underneath the surface of our time, and money excuses like fear, fear of failure, fear of disappointment, imposter syndrome, etc... It is often easier to blame the more superficial, yet tangible obstacles like time and money than to take a deep look within ourselves at what is really causing us to say NO to something we say we want.

In addition, time and money are often acceptable excuses in our society, so they are easy to fall back on with little to no judgement from ourselves or others. They are relatively safe excuses. However, if becoming a Wise Leader is important to you, you will need to be willing to dive deep to discover the real reasons you are saying no, and open yourself up to the way revealing itself.

Strategies for Overcoming Time and Money Excuses

- Take actual stock of your time. Create a timesheet and see where your time is going. Are you as efficient as you could be? Are you actually giving time to less important things (like scrolling on social media) than the things you say you are committed to? What could you shuffle, change, or give up in order to make room for your leadership activities?
- Now that you have identified some holes (even if only 5 minutes), start putting it in your calendar and give yourself a start date to begin devoting this time to your Wise Leadership.

- If money is the issue, evaluate your money situation. Look money in the eye, and take stock of where it is going. Is it going to the things that are most important and/or necessary? Is there something that needs re-arranging?

- To be a Wise Leader, what do you need money for? Is it fundraising? Is it running for office? Is it hiring a coach to help develop you as a leader? Evaluate, and prioritize what activities are most important to spend money on right now in order to accomplish your goals. Evaluate the value of each. Research if there are other options. Decide what is important, what isn't, what you can find a free resource for, or how you can generate the money you need.

- Write about your excuses. Why are time and money an obstacle to your Wise Leadership? Ask yourself, is this true? Keep writing.

- What if time and money were not an obstacle, then what? Write about what you would do next if time and money were not an obstacle. See what other thoughts and feelings come up. Imagine yourself moving forward in your Wise Leadership. Notice any resistance or fear. Keep writing to uncover any hidden obstacles. Use the strategies in the other chapters to overcome them.

- Be open to solutions and opportunities. Choose to believe that there is always an answer, always a way. Ask for guidance or support. Commit to what is most important to you, and be open to the way presenting itself.

- For a hypnosis track to help you release your limiting beliefs about money, go to www.drdonnamarino.com/unleash

Summary

Time and money are probably the most common excuses that keep people from taking action. Often, they are just that, excuses. If you are using time and money as an excuse to keep you from stepping into your Wise Leadership, try the exercises above to get to the root cause and to honestly evaluate your situation. Time and money are a dead-end excuse that closes you off to opportunity. If you want to claim your leadership, you are going to have to let them go and open up to solutions.

Chapter 9: Sabotage (Bucking the Status Quo, and Homeostasis)

So here it is, sabotage. This is the thing. You are used to being you, and so is everyone else who knows you. When you begin to shift and change, especially when you begin to expand, you are probably going to get scared. ...and so will your friends and family.

Growth is scary. It changes you. It stretches you. It moves you into unknown territory. If it didn't, you would just be in your safety zone, and not your growth zone. To become a Wise Leader, you are going to have to grow. It's not so much changing who you are as stepping into the fullest expression of you. Let that sink in for a minute. _It's not about changing who you are, but it's about stepping into the fullest expression of you._

Up until now, you may have been playing small or safe. You may have been hiding in the shadows or quietly serving others. But Wise Leadership means taking the lead, standing up for what you believe in, and taking control of your life. It means finding your voice, right? It means being visible, and that scares a lot of people.

So what happens when we get scared by our own expansion? Sabotage.

Sabotage is an attempt from unseen forces to course-correct back to the status quo or homeostasis. Remember when we spoke about homeostasis and Imposter Syndrome? Think of Imposter Syndrome as mental sabotage to keep you in your old identity in order to keep things "normal." Not only do our bodies and brains like homeostasis, but so do our relationships.

Sabotage can come in many forms. It can be the car breaking down on the way to that important meeting or your kid getting sick as you are about to leave for a leadership conference. It can be that friend who tells you to blow off that PTA meeting or networking event to go have a glass of wine or it can be old patterns of thinking, feeling, and behaving that keep you in your old ways of doing things in your comfort zone.

Sabotage is to be expected. It is going to happen whether it is of your own doing, your subconscious, someone else, or what seems like an act of God. Everyone I have ever known who has made a significant change to their life has experienced it. The more you accept it as par for the course, the less you will get caught up in the head games of "maybe I'm not supposed to be doing this after all" or "maybe I'm not good enough" or "maybe I was wrong about this."

Sure, I believe that there are signs, and sometimes we are being told to detour, but in every case, I know people have been challenged to stay on their course. Call it a test, call it a coincidence, call it a sign, persistence always overcomes. In the words of one of my own coaches, it's commitment, consistency, and investment that gets you to your goals. So when sabotage rears its ugly head, instead of saying this means I should quit, take it as a sign to dig in your heels and demonstrate your commitment, consistency, and investment in your own leadership, your own ambition.

This means developing a certain mental and emotional toughness. No one enjoys the sabotage experience, but the consequence of avoiding it is not growing, not going after what you want. …and if you retreat in the face of sabotage all you do is undo all the work you have done to get there when what you want is probably just around the corner. You see, many times, sabotage screams the loudest just before you get what you want. Think of it as a roller coaster. Just hold on tight, buckle up, and scream if you have to, but enjoy the ride because everything you want is just on the other side.

Now, you're going to experience hard days. You are going to experience fear, doubt, imposter syndrome. We talked about all of that. Sometimes being a leader means taking a few arrows in your backside as you charge out in front. Your job is to lick your wounds and get back on track as soon as possible. It's to make your recovery time quicker with each injury and to learn from your experiences. It is to not give up in the face of obstacles. It is to embrace the challenge even when it stinks. It's okay to acknowledge that it stinks. You just keep going.

Conquering Sabotage

- Reviewing the exercises in Chapter 5, The Power of Purpose can be very helpful when dealing with sabotage. It is important to remind yourself of your "Why?" during times like these so that you can reconnect with your passion and motivation to keep ongoing.

- You might also track your sabotage for evidence of breakthroughs. For example, when you think sabotage is occurring, instead of getting riled up, become a scientist. Look at it objectively. Write down the date, and time, what happened, and what was significant about the event. Then sit and wait for your big breakthrough. When it comes, write it down. Notice how soon after your sabotage, something positive happened that put you closer to your goal. Notice any other correlations in how the two events are connected. For example, perhaps the car broke down, and it turns out the tow truck guy is a cousin of the person that is now giving you an opportunity to speak on their stage. Take notice of coincidences and document them. You will begin to show your brain the evidence that it is okay.

- Creating a special mantra or affirmation for these particular times can also be helpful. Something like "This too shall pass" or "Something better is on its way" can help diffuse the feelings of frustration and instill hope.

- Visualize yourself on the other side of this sabotage experience. Visualize yourself fully accomplishing your goal. Visualize yourself in the fullest expression of you as a Wise Leader. Hold on to that feeling with all of your senses, and anchor it into your body in the solar plexus or heart. Tap into this feeling whenever you feel overwhelmed or like giving up. For a guided visualization, go to www.drdonnamarino.com/unleash

- When you need a little added mental or emotional toughness, just ask yourself what would the best version of me do? You may have a name for her or a title, like CEO, but tap into that energy, and ask her for guidance. Act as if you are her already.

Summary

Whenever you buck the status quo and turn homeostasis on its head, you can expect to have sabotage come up. It may originate from our subconscious objections that don't like what we are doing, from the loved ones that are frightened by our expansion, or from what seem like acts of God. The sooner you can accept sabotage as a part of the process of up-leveling into your Wise Leadership, the better off you will be. Once you have accepted it as a part of the process, you can begin using the tools in this chapter to get you through to the other side to where your next level begins.

Chapter 10: Your Tribe (Or Lack There Of)

Your tribe. Do you have one? Do they support you? Will they cheer you on as you expand into your next levels of leadership, or will it scare them? Will they feel left behind? Will they understand what you are trying to do, or will they unconsciously sabotage or results because they don't get it?

These are important and tough questions. Many women, as they rise in leadership, think they have a tribe, and find out that they do not. This can be a harsh reality for many. Not everyone is called to lead like you are. Not everyone gets it. Not everyone understands the amount of personal growth and transformation it takes to stand in your leadership power. Some of your friends and even family are going to think you're nuts. They won't get it. They may even say things like you've changed, or you're not fun anymore. They are going to want you to stay the same because it makes them feel better about who they are. They may be threatened by your success, and you will have to make some tough decisions. Do you keep playing small to hold on to old relationships, or do you fulfill your calling, your potential, and possibly leave some relationships behind. The thought of this may be scaring you right now, but it's important we face it now, so that you will be prepared when the time comes, and you have to make these choices because you will have to make them. That's what a leader does.

Now, I'm not saying that you are going to lose everyone that is important to you. Take a deep breath. But there will be relationships that you outgrow, and new ones that you have to cultivate. You are not going to be able to be a part of the Debbie Downer club sitting around drinking wine, and complaining, blaming, or gossiping about other people. Nope. That is not leadership behavior, and it will not get you to where you want to be. Does it mean you have to dump them on their ear? No, but the relationship may change. I have a friend Tracie, who puts it this way; there are 2-minute friends, 20-minute friends, 2-hour friends, etc... What does she mean by this? You have to put boundaries around friends that are not good for you. This goes for family members too. You may not cut them out of your life completely, but they may only get 2 minutes of your time if all they do is gripe. As a leader, you have to be solution focused. You have to be protective of your mind and your energy from negative and derailing influences. This means limiting your contact with negative or energy-draining people. You not only owe that to yourself but to all the people you influence as a leader.

I know you are asking, "But what about when it's my family or someone I live with? I can't just get rid of my mother or my spouse." While it's true that family relationships can be more complicated and more challenging to put boundaries around, it is also not impossible. There is always a solution. To start with, you have to protect your dreams. I want you to think of your ambitions as a baby chick that you have to care for, protect, and nurture. You are not going to put it in harm's way, which means not exposing it to others that could harm it. Only share your big visions with those that can see it too. Those that support you and will nurture the flame of your desire. Keep your visions close to your vest until you know someone is also a visionary and can help cheer you on. Don't share them with those that will only throw negativity or doubt or a bucket of cold water on the flame of your desire. Don't let them hurt your baby chick.

Another strategy that you can use, and that I have taught many a client is that when you know you are going to come into contact with someone that is difficult, negative, or conflict seeking imagine in your mind that you have a beautiful bubble of golden white light surrounding you that prevents any of that from coming in, and reaching you. All of the negativity or conflict just bounces right off. You can expand your bubble to be as big as you need it to be, or you can contract to allow other positive influences in, but it is there to protect you and your energy. Don't allow others to penetrate your bubble without your permission. It is your job to keep your bubble intact. It is the bubble's job to protect you, the leader.

It's going to take some time and practice to get good at not letting others enter your bubble or impact your thoughts and energy around your goal; especially if you are someone who is sensitive to criticism or a people-pleaser (always wanting others approval), which is very common among women. So, have some grace for yourself. Be compassionate. This is a process. It doesn't happen overnight. Being hard on yourself is only going to make the process take longer.

Do your best to be an objective observer. For example, say something like this instead, "Oh, I see there where Jerry said, 'you think you can do that?,' and I allowed fear and doubt to creep in, and stopped working on that goal for a few days. Next time, I will have to strengthen my bubble, and let those comments bounce off of me."

As a leader, you are going to have to get good at being the objective observer. Women are emotional creatures, and this is not a bad thing. In fact, our emotions are a guidance system that can be trusted when we are functioning from our highest self. But emotions that are connected to old stories or wounds will not serve us in our decision-making. This is when we need the objective observer, not the wounded child, to help us see clearly what the next step is. A great way to practice the objective observer is through meditation.

Another way is to journal about these highly charged situations as an outsider. Write down just the facts. Take the emotion out of it and observe what happened. You may have to write the emotional story first in order to get to this level of detachment, but this practice will help you see objectively what occurred, and what you can do differently next time.

This is a part of growing your emotional intelligence, which is key for being a good leader. You not only have to learn to be able to manage your own emotions effectively, especially those concerning your leadership goals; but you will also need to be able to manage, perceive, and respond to the emotions of those you wish to lead from an objective leadership position, not from a reactive wounded child. We have all seen "leaders" who have done that. It is not pretty, and it is not leadership. This is why doing your own personal work is key to being a good leader. Nobody needs a child in leadership.

So now that you have been culling your tribe and eliminating nay-sayers, "Negative Nancys" and "Debbie Downers." It is time to build your tribe of solution-focused, powerful, collaborative, and creative men and women. Yes, I say men and women because you are going to need both to get you where you want to be. It is not just women's work to get into leadership. We need men on our side as well to help open doors, share their knowledge, and be our champions. We have to work together to see this happen.

Assembling your tribe, as you begin to up-level, is very important to getting you to where you want to be. Some of it will happen very organically as you start attracting new people into your sphere of influence who are drawn to your new energy and ambition. This is a great time to put your focus on what you are gaining over what you may be losing.

You should consciously think about the types of people you want in your tribe. What are their psychographics? In other words, how do they think, act, feel? What are their morals, ethics, ambitions, motivators? What is their role in your tribe? Get clear first not on specific people you want to have in your inner circle, but the types of people that you want to have.

You may want a cheerleader on your team that is always there to lift you up. You may want a mentor or advisor who is a private confidant that has gone down this road already and can share their experience with you. I'm telling you; you are going to want a sponsor. That is, someone who is a public advocate for you and is willing to use their power and influence to help you get where you want to be. But think about all the players that you want on your team; peers, collaborators, challengers, coaches, connectors, etc… that can help bring out your best ideas, support you, encourage you, make connections with you, help you stretch, and grow without bringing you down, and offer opportunities. Write all of this down. As we have discussed before, the act of writing it down makes it that much more powerful.

Your brain begins to see it, rather than just having it swirl around in your head. It becomes more real.

Now, think about the type of person you would like to be in someone else's tribe. Remember, it goes both ways, and you want to be a giver in the world, not a taker. Givers form better relationships and develop more opportunities. They demonstrate their value to others and often end up top of mind because of that. But you have to do it from a pure heart, not just with the thought of what you are going to get out of it. Do it knowing that your giving will be returned in some way, but it is not a direct 1:1 ratio. What you receive may not come directly from the person that you gave to, but it will come back.

However, I am not talking about over-giving here or being a martyr. That is not what this is about. I'm talking about being of high service for others, being a valued member of the tribe. It should feel good to you when you give. If you feel anger, resentment, or burdened, then it is not high service, and you are probably over-giving. Don't do that. You should feel energized, not depleted. You are sharing value. There is a mutual exchange of energy. That is the type of giving I am talking about. You have to be the type of tribe member you would want to have in your inner circle. Then you will attract others who want the same.

While your tribe is going to be essential to reaching your leadership potential, do not fret if it is not assembled already. Many of you are probably thinking, I don't have a cheerleader or a sponsor. It's okay. These shifts won't happen overnight, but they will happen as you evolve into your leadership role. They will happen even quicker and easier if you set the clear intentions of who you want to draw in. Be as specific as possible when you are writing down your wish list of your tribe members. If a specific person comes to mind as you write your list, engage with them, and see what happens. But stay open-minded to the result. Try not to attach to the outcome of having this specific person on your tribe but stay clear on finding someone like him/her or even better. It's okay to go after someone you perceive as a perfect member of your tribe. Just try not to get stuck on the idea that it has to be that exact person. There could be someone even better out there for you.

Strategies for Creating Your Tribe

- Create a list of the people you interact with regularly and write an honest evaluation of whether they are a 2-minute, 20-minute, 2-hour, or 2+ day person. Separate into two lists: potential tribe members and non-tribe members.

- Write down how you are going to set appropriate boundaries with each person on the non-tribe member list. Then write each person a letter thanking them for your past relationship and establishing the boundaries of this new relationship. This is for your use only, not to be sent. It's to demonstrate gratitude and boundaries to your subconscious and conscious mind so that the relationship begins to shift. You may choose to write goodbye letters to relationships that you feel must be ended. Again, this is for your own use.

- Label the relationships that are potential members of your tribe with the role you perceive for them, such as: cheerleader; sponsor; advocate; mentor; connector; etc..

- Create a list of your dream team. Not specifically who they are, but the roles you want to see filled, and the characteristics of the people that will fulfill those roles. Think of it as a job description that is very clear about the type of person(s) you want on your team. Their skills may be a part of it, but you want to get very clear on their psychographics. In other words, how they think, feel, and act. What makes them a good member of the tribe? How will they help you reach your goals?

- If specific names come to mind, you can put them next to the role and accompanying list of characteristics; but also write "or someone even better."

- Write your own job description as a tribe member. What is your role in your own tribe? What is your role when serving in someone else's tribe? What do you have to offer?

- Go to www.drdonnamarino.com/unleash to download a hypnosis track to help you attract your tribe to you.

Summary

Your tribe can help make you or help break you when you are up-leveling your leadership. They can be an obstacle to your success, or they can be an elevator. There are going to be people that can't handle your expansion, your personal growth, and the full expression of who you are. That is okay. I understand that it may cause you to grieve the loss of those relationships, but everyone who has gone through this process has had this experience. You get to choose how to handle it. Do you sacrifice your potential so that others stay comfortable? Or do you grow and allow yourself to impact the world in the way that you are called to? It's totally up to you.

Leaders have to make tough decisions. It's part of being a leader, and it often starts with your own inner circle. A leader needs a tribe, a council, a board, call it what you will, but you need an inner circle that has your back, that believes in you, that can challenge you to keep growing, that can open new doors to opportunity, that can advise you, and guide you, and that helps you reach your fullest potential. Cultivating your tribe will be one of your first acts of leadership.

Part III: Implementation: What does this look like in real life?

Introduction

In Part I, you learned the five principles of Wise Leadership: Claim Your Leadership, Unleash Your Ambition, Find Your Voice, Lift Each Other Up, and The Power of Purpose.

In Part II, you learned about the obstacles to expect to arise as you move into Wise Leadership and how to overcome them.

Now, in Part III, we focus on implementation. None of this will do you any good unless you actually take it out of your head and into your life. People spend money all the time on books, courses, retreats, seminars etc.... to grow and change, but only about 2% actually implement what they learn. I want to change that. I want YOU to change that. That is why I have gone through so much effort to actually teach you how to overcome the obstacles and to create the additional audio tracks, companion workbook, and card deck to support you in the process.

One of my former clients once asked me, "Why didn't all of the other people I have worked with (therapists, coaches, mentors etc....) ever tell me that it's not the time we spend together that counts, but the daily work every other day implementing what I've learned in our time together that really makes the change?" I don't know why no one had ever told him this before, but I want you to pay close attention now because I am telling you. When you put down this book, if you don't do the exercises recommended, if you don't use the supplemental materials, if you don't do the daily work, then nothing changes.

If you want to be a Wise Leader, you have to decide that you already are one, and then you have to do the work every day to BE one. As I said earlier on in the book, it's about embodiment. If you do not embody it, which means living it, then you might as well have not read the book. Make the decision now before moving on to Part III, to live what you learn, and to be one of the Wise Leaders in the world today.

I'm rooting for you.

Dr. Donna

Chapter 11: At Home

Wise Leadership starts at home. Actually, it begins with you. You can't lead others if you are not leading yourself first. How well are you leading yourself right now? Do you have daily rituals and routines that support your personal growth, your health, your embodiment of leadership?

Here's a checklist of activities that I recommend doing every day to support yourself and your goals.
- Exercise
- Drinking at least 6-8 glasses of water a day
- 6-8 hours of sleep a night
- Nutritious foods at the right times for your body
- Limit your intake of caffeine, alcohol, and sugar
- Getting fresh air on days when the weather allows
- Journaling
- Meditating
- Affirmations
- Visualization
- Reading or listening to inspirational material
- Practicing gratitude
- Reading your goals

How many can you check off right now that you are already doing? Which ones need your attention and can be added into your day?

If you are not already using a daily planner, I highly recommend doing so. Schedule these activities into your day and honor them just as you would a doctor's appointment. They should become part of your non-negotiables. This will help lay the foundation for your success by creating a healthy nervous system, a healthy body, and a healthy mind.

Now, I know it looks like a lot, and you are probably saying you do not have the time for this. Once these become part of your daily routine, though, it will not feel like a lot. Plus, several of these will be integrated throughout your day, and do not take additional time. Many of these will only take a few minutes. Trust me, every Wise Leader I know has rituals and routines that support their mind, body, and soul so that they can show up as the leader they are called to be without resentment, burnout, or martyr syndrome. Being a Wise Leader means being wise with yourself first. That's also the first step towards claiming your leadership at home.

Claiming Your Leadership at Home

Who do you consider the leader of your home now? Is it you or someone else? What do you think it looks like to be the leader at home? What would it mean to you to be the leader at home? It is important for you to take the time to really ponder these questions and know your answers. Everyone's home is different, and what leadership means to you in your home is going to be different than someone else's, so it's important that YOU know what it means for you, and the people you live with.

Once you know the answers to these questions, you can begin to dive deeper. You can ask yourself, where am I not leading at home that I think I should be or that I want to be? This could be your finances, or where to take the next family vacation, or any number of decisions and activities where you feel like perhaps you have taken a backseat or been more submissive. There is no right or wrong answer here nor any blame, shame, or guilt to be had. This is just an assessment and an opportunity for you to shift into a fuller expression of yourself. It is not to make you feel bad for any past decisions or behaviors, but just to ask, "where have I not claimed my leadership in the past, and where do I need to start doing it now?"

So, for example, claiming your leadership in the home might be becoming an equal partner in financial planning if you aren't already. It could also be being more involved in decision making regarding certain aspects of the home, the family, or even shared leisure time. It could also be delegating tasks and responsibilities so that they are more evenly shared. Claiming your leadership is not necessarily about taking on more; sometimes, it's about taking on less.

Even though more than 50% of families have two parents working outside of the home, studies still show that women shoulder the majority of the homecare, and childcare responsibilities, even when they also work outside the home. Wise Leaders know they cannot do it all, and they know how to delegate. A Wise Leader knows the value of her time, her areas of expertise, and what she needs to let go of to make room for the areas where she really shines. Claiming your leadership could mean hiring someone to clean the house or help prep meals or having older children do their own laundry and help with cooking.

Claiming your leadership as a Wise Leader means assessing the situation and knowing where you need to step up and where you need to step down. Consider it like being promoted. You can't do all the same tasks you used to do because you have new, bigger tasks that only you can do. Congrats!

Unleashing Your Ambition at Home

What does unleashing your ambition look like at home? In other words, what are those new, bigger tasks you want to take on that only you can do?

There are so many different ways that unleashing your ambition at home can look. For example, it could be a home project you always wanted to take on like renovating a room of the house or building a garden; or it could be a personal project like a new skill you wanted to learn, like gourmet cooking or self-defense. It really could be anything that helps you stand in your leadership and be a fuller expression of yourself.

What have you always wanted to do that you thought, "I can't do that because the family needs me" or "I'm not strong enough" or "that seems too hard or scary." It's time to shed those excuses and go after what you want.

There is one more way to unleash your ambition at home that has nothing to do with home projects or personal activities. That is to share your career and community ambitions with your family. Maybe you don't have a home project you want to do or a new skill you are dying to learn. Sharing your other ambitions with your family is a way of unleashing your ambition at home. Your family can see what drives you, what excites you, and what your dreams are. It is especially important for our sons and daughters to see their mother's ambitions if we want to see more women in leadership. We want our children to see a woman's ambitions as normal, and healthy. We want them to be excited by them too. If we really want to see gender parity in leadership, it starts at home.

Whatever your ambitions are, let those closest to you (and who will support you) see them. Be proud of them. It's who you are being called to be. You wouldn't have been given these desires if you weren't meant to act upon them. Leadership, by definition, is about influence. A Wise Leader uses that influence for good. For women who have children, there is no one she will influence more. Show your strength and courage. Your children need you to.

But whether you are a mother or not, the children of the world are looking up to you. They see you. They admire you. They want to be like you. Your actions do matter, and when they see you Claim Your Leadership and Unleash your Ambition, you pave the way for them to do it to.

Finding Your Voice at Home

Have you ever noticed how your voice can change depending on whom you are speaking with? Like when you get on a call with customer service, your voice sounds one way; but if you get on a call with a friend or loved one, it sounds another way, right? So, finding your voice at home may be different than finding your voice out in the world. Some of you have no problem with finding your voice at home. For others, it's actually easier for you to have your voice at work. Take some time now to think about this. What is your voice like at home? Do you hold back, or do you say what you need to? Does it depend on the situation? Does it depend on the emotion? Are you conflict avoidant at home or with certain people in the home, but not others? This is a great exercise to really explore your communication with the people you live with. Where does it thrive, and where does it need work? I recommend taking some time to journal your answers to these questions now and then come back.

••

What did you discover about yourself?

Once you have identified the areas that you have been holding back, and your need to find more of your voice, you can begin working on them. For many people, this is going to be in the area of conflict resolution versus conflict avoidance. Many people are conflict avoidant, especially women, and especially with those they love the most. Obviously, this is a generalization and will not apply to everyone. I do know plenty of men who are also conflict-avoidant, especially with their partners. However, due to the socialization of women to be "good girls," they tend to struggle slightly more with this issue.

When it comes to finding your voice in conflict, here are some recommendations:

- Talk to the person you are having difficulty expressing yourself at a time when you are not having conflict. Let them know that you have come to recognize that you have a pattern of conflict avoidance. If you feel comfortable, share with this person, what about conflict makes you frightened or uncomfortable. Discuss your ideas for how you are going to work on your avoidance, and how you would like to be instead. If possible, come up with a strategy together of how you can address conflict when it occurs. Set guidelines and boundaries for resolving conflict, such as:
    - Do not try to address the conflict in the heat of the moment, but rather come back to it for a discussion when both of you are calm and ready to talk.

- Allow either person to request a break if the conversation becomes too heated. Agree on how long the break should be and set a timer. Come back to talk again or request another break if still not ready.

- When conflict occurs, and you are not yet ready to talk about it, write about it. Write everything you would like to say, no matter what it is. Get it all out, and then destroy it.

- Make "I" statements: I feel angry when you say the house is a mess because…

- Avoid using absolute language such as always, and never, whenever possible.

- Absolutely **NO** name-calling.

The practice of finding your voice at home will be supported by your daily affirmation practice, especially saying your affirmations aloud. Also, by taking note and patting yourself on the back each time that you voice your thoughts and opinions in a constructive way, especially in situations in which you may not have before. Every time that we consciously reward ourselves for a behavior, we get a shot of dopamine from our brain, which makes us feel good, and makes us more likely to do that behavior again. So, don't be shy about congratulating yourself and celebrating your wins.

Lifting Each Other Up at Home

Lifting each other up at home means supporting each other's ambitions, goals, and dreams, and acts of Wise Leadership. Your home should be your haven. It should be your safe place filled with the people, pets, and things you love. I know it won't always feel that way, but that should be the intention of a home. The place you can fully be yourself and be loved and accepted.

The way we do that is by creating an environment where you lift each other up. That should be the norm in a Wise Leader's home. If leadership is about influence, then Wise Leadership at home is definitely about helping each member be the best version of themselves. If we are knocking each other down, calling each other names, criticizing or mocking someone's dreams or ambitions, then we are not using our influence for good, and we are not acting as a Wise Leader in our home.

What are some actions you can take today to lift up the other people in your home? …And remember it starts with you. If you live alone or if you are the one who needs lifting up today, then start with you. When you are feeling better and have something left to give, look around you, and start lifting up those around you. But a Wise Leader does not cut people down, even when they don't have the energy to lift them up. It is better to be neutral or to take some time alone if you can't be an uplifter.

The Power of Purpose at Home

Although every day will not be easy, knowing your WHY in the home should be an easy one. As I've said, our homes should be our haven. We all want our homes to be a place of happiness, comfort, and joy. Being a Wise Leader should help us create that.

Ask yourself these questions:
- Why do I want to be a Wise Leader at home?
- What does that mean to me?
- Why is it important for my own well-being to be a Wise Leader?
- Why is it important for the other people in my home for me to be a Wise Leader?
- What would be different about my home life if I showed up as a Wise Leader?
- What is my big Why for being a Wise Leader at home?

Once you have the answers to your questions, write your BIG WHY as a mission statement for your Wise Leadership at home, and post it somewhere you can see every day, like the bathroom mirror. Make sure to read this when you have those days that make it hard to stay in your Wise Leadership. It will help reconnect you and ground you to your purpose.

Summary

Being a Wise Leader at home means integrating the principles of Wise Leadership into your home life with yourself and your family. It all starts with you. If you aren't taking care of yourself, then you won't have the proper foundation to lead from.

First, you have to create the daily rituals and routines that support your overall well-being, as well as your leadership goals. Wise Leadership is a daily practice, not a once in a while thing. To truly embody the Wise Leader, you have to work at it every day; but it does get easier over time as your daily practices become second-nature. You can't stop doing them, or you will go back to your old ways, but they will become like brushing your teeth, and you will want to do them and notice the impact when you miss it. As you lay this foundation for your own success, you will begin implementing the 5 Principles of Wise Leadership. You'll have a chance to define them for yourself as to what this looks like in your home. Some possibilities include:

- Claiming your Leadership might mean becoming more involved in the household finances or in planning the family vacation, but it might also be delegating household chores to others to make more room for your leadership activities.

- Unleashing your ambition could mean taking on a household project like renovating a room or picking up a new skill, like self-defense, but it could also be sharing your ambitions for your career and your life with your family members.

- Finding your voice at home may be getting more comfortable with conflict resolution or speaking up on topics that you usually shied away from.

- Lifting each other up in any home means that you support one another in your visions, your goals, and your ambitions. For the home to be a safe haven, this is a must. If you want each member of the household to reach their full potential, you must lift each other up, not cut each other down. This is not in an "everybody gets a gold star" kind of way, but in a way that is genuinely supportive of ideas, emotions, and goals.

- The Power of Purpose is there to help you stay committed to being a Wise Leader in your home. On the days where it feels like too much or too hard, your WHY is what will get you through. Being a Wise Leader in your home should create more harmony, more joy, more courage, and more peace. Take time to write down all your reasons for why you want to be a Wise Leader at home, and be sure to put them in a place that you can refer back to, especially on the tough days.

For more help embodying Wise Leadership in your home, go to www.drdonnamarino.com/unleash for a guided visualization to help see yourself as the Wise Leader at home.

Chapter 12: At Work

Think of your leadership influence as moving through concentric circles with you at the center, then your home, your work, your community, and finally, the world. Once you are leading yourself and your home, you can begin to expand outwards into your career. In truth, these circles will influence one another, and at times be bidirectional. However, you really need to master the art of leading yourself and your home to be as effective as possible in the outside world. Maybe you are already in a leadership position at work, and maybe you are not, yet. You might desire to be in a leadership position, or you may be happy where you are. No matter where you are at in your career, this chapter will teach you how to show up as a Wise Leader in whatever role you choose.

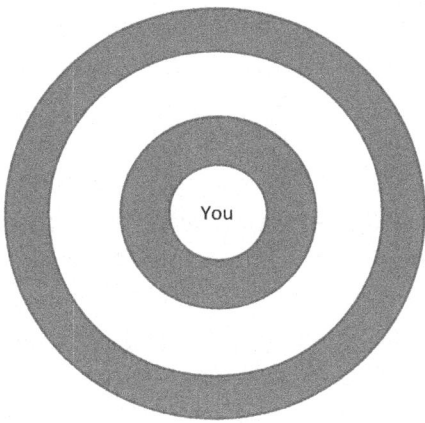

Claiming Your Leadership at Work

Many women cringe at the idea of claiming their leadership at work. To them, it may sound bossy, pushy, or arrogant. They may be thinking, "Who am I to claim my leadership?" Remember the Marianne Williamson poem from Chapter 2? The question actually is, "Who are you not too?"

Funny enough, the ones that are usually the most concerned about this are the ones that have a far way to go before being any of those things. They are usually the ones that are so far from bossy, pushy, or arrogant that they would never even cross that line. It's the ones that never worry about it, that might need to give it some thought here and there, not the ones that are terrified by the idea.

It's true that strong women at work run the risk of getting mislabeled a b*&#h. We have seen this happen, but that does not have to be the case. In fact, if we let fears of being labeled as such deter us from pursuing leadership, then that label is doing just what others intend, keeping you in "your place." In this section, we will talk about ways to claim your leadership that are proactive and assertive; but not aggressive. But before we do that, I want to make a note about race.

Note: I, as a white woman, will make no claims to knowing the experiences of those in this country who do not share my skin color. That would be crass and unfair. When I was giving my talk on Wise Leadership before, an African-American woman in the audience made me aware of her unique struggles to claiming her leadership and finding her voice as an African-American woman. She explained to me the risks of coming across as a stereotype of "an angry black woman." My heart ached for her struggle, but I cannot pretend to know it. If you are reading this book and are faced with some of those same issues in the workplace, please know that I hope we see a time when that no longer happens and that you, the only expert of your own experience, will know the way to apply these principles that is best for you. I mean absolutely no disrespect in any of my suggestions or recommendations.

The first step once again starts with your mind. You have to decide 100% that you are a leader and not just any leader, but a Wise Leader. You are someone who influences others positively. You are someone who makes decisions that impact others. You are thoughtful about your impact. You use your gifts and talents to the benefit of your company, your colleagues, your coworkers, and yourself. You care about your outcomes and put forth your best effort. You speak up when you have a question, a comment, or a solution to offer. You acknowledge others' hard work and intentional efforts. You volunteer for exciting opportunities. Can you say yes to most, if not all, of these? If so, it's time to accept and own that you are a Wise Leader. When you see yourself as a Wise Leader at work, others will begin to as well. As always, it starts with you.

When you are at work, carry yourself like a leader, dress like a leader, and make decisions like a leader. If you get stuck on something, ask yourself, "what would the Wise Leader do in this situation?" Keep channeling the Wise Leader within you, and reconnecting with that part of yourself. This will help you embody her.

<u>Unleashing Your Ambition at Work</u>

Once you have claimed your leadership internally, you can start expressing it externally by going after what you want. This may be volunteering for new opportunities or bringing your creative ideas to your boss. It is important to share your long-term vision with the people above you who can help you get there. Don't be afraid to reach big or to suggest a new way of doing things. Don't talk yourself out of your ideas and ambitions. Let them flow.

Research shows that women apply for jobs and promotions at least twenty percent less than men and that they feel they have to meet 100% of the hiring criteria before they apply. In contrast, men will apply if they meet 60% of the criteria. While gender differences in promotions and leadership cannot be denied, women have to stop cutting themselves off at the knees and go for it. If you don't throw your hat in the ring, then you a part of the problem.

Now I know that you have your reasons. Many women are afraid of moving up the ladder at work because of how it could affect their home life. They may be concerned about their career taking them away from their family or even how their spouse will respond if they start to make more money than them. The thing is if we don't go for it, then we'll never know if these concerns were even valid in the first place. We also rob ourselves and others when we stifle our full potential.

If your heart is calling out for more challenge, more influence, and more impact, don't hold back. You can always say no or make a detour. No decision is forever. What is it that you really want in your career? How can you show up as a Wise Leader? How can you be the fullest expression of yourself at work? How would your work culture be different if you unleashed your ambition?

Take time to visualize yourself in the roles you desire, and then go after them. Build your circle of people at work who support your visions and let them know your ambitions. Begin gathering mentors, sponsors, and advocates who can help you get where you want to be. If there isn't anyone in your office, then look outside your office. Every great leader has a great team of advisors and experts who can help them get where they want to be. This will take an investment on your part of either time, money, or both; but no one fulfills their highest ambitions alone. Find the people that can help you get there.

Finding Your Voice at Work

To be a Wise Leader at work, you have to have a voice, you have to use that voice as a positive influence, and you have to be a solid decision-maker.

When considering your voice, I want you to think of your voice as your leadership style. How will you convey your thoughts, ideas, and requests to others? How do you want to be defined as a leader? What are your values?

For example, I had a client who was an attorney and CEO of a large financial institution. Over lunch one day, she told me, "I can't win. My board (made up of older Caucasian gentlemen) tells me I'm too lenient, but my staff (made of a more diverse group of men and women) tell me I'm too bitchy." She was frustrated but ultimately decided to not worry about what others thought or said, and to focus on developing her own style of effective communication that delivered results. She was a highly effective and competent leader with little employee turnover.

This can be a common frustration, though for women in executive positions. The stereotypes are one extreme or the other. Clearly, she could not have been both extremes. The bottom line is you will never please everyone, so stop trying. Listen to the opinions of people you trust and find your own way. You have to lead from your own heart, your own wisdom, and your own unique voice. You can learn from others and their styles, but you still have to find your own way.

When you do find your voice, you have to use it to effect change in a positive way. Speak up in meetings when you have an idea. No more slinking into the corner. No more waiting so long for your turn to speak that you never say anything. Jump on in! If your being polite (by never interrupting) means that you are not being heard, you might want to reconsider your politeness. It may just be better to ask forgiveness than permission on that one.

It's time to use your voice to speak up, initiate change, and contribute value. The Wise Leader uses her power, her strength, and her voice to improve the company, the workplace, her co-workers, and colleagues' experiences, and much more. She makes decisions in alignment with the highest good for all, and she does this with confidence and courage. That is what finding your voice in the workplace looks like, and you don't have to be a CEO to do it.

Lifting Each Other Up at Work

I think it goes without saying that if you want to be a Wise Leader at work, you have to lift others up. After all, being a leader is not really about you; it's about how you influence and impact others. How can you possibly be a positive leader if you aren't lifting up the people around you?
That does not mean that you condone "bad" behavior from subordinates or give everyone a gold star. But what it does mean is seeing the strengths and potential in others and helping them achieve their goals. It means having an interest in what motivates them, excites them, and what their long-term goals are.

It also means focusing on collaboration in the workplace over competition. That means not undercutting your colleagues, not gossiping, and never rooting for anyone else to fail.

In order to lift each other up and stay out of competition, you have to have the right mindset. Being a Wise Leader means staying in a mindset of abundance, believing that there is plenty of opportunity, money, prestige, etc… to go around. When you get stuck in the scarcity mindset, that is when competition is amplified, and in-fighting begins. In-fighting often leads to a hostile work environment and definitely is not Wise Leadership. The Wise Leader encourages collaboration, acknowledges, and rewards other's successes, and encourages others to keep striving.

No matter what role or title the Wise Leader actually has at the office, the Wise Leader works to bring out the best in others.

The Power of Purpose at Work

The Wise Leader knows that her work is an extension of her purpose. If your work is not an extension of your purpose or calling, then I suggest that you re-evaluate. While it is possible to fulfill your purpose outside of work, most people find that fulfilling their purpose through their work brings them more joy, more overall life satisfaction, and more fulfillment.

The work you do should allow you to fully express your gifts, strengths, and talents. It should have meaning to you. It should matter to you. There are plenty of people who work jobs, but the Wise Leader works their calling. A job is just a paycheck, and it is the right thing to do if that's what you need to do to support yourself and your family. Sadly, for those in poverty or survival mode, and need their most basic needs met, a job may be the right place for them right now. But I'm talking about the Wise Leader. The Wise Leader is looking at the top of Maslow's hierarchy, not the bottom, and is asking, "What is my unique contribution to the world?"

It is my belief that you are given your unique set of talents, strengths, and passions, specifically so that you can fulfill your purpose. I think they are like clues to what your purpose is. If you were to draw a Venn diagram and write all of your strengths on one side and then all the things that you are passionate about on the other side; your purpose would be in the overlap of those two circles, where your strengths and passions come together.

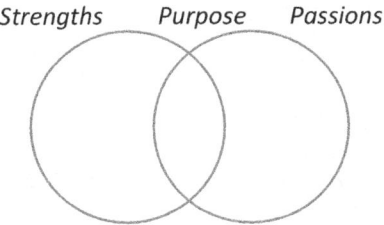

To be a Wise Leader, you need to know your purpose. You need to know "what is it all for?" As we've talked about before, it is that WHY that is going to get you through the hard times. It is that WHY that is going to be the basis of your decision making and your leadership. Everything flows from your WHY.

Your WHY doesn't have to be like anyone else's. It doesn't have to be a grand gesture of changing the world, although it could be. Your WHY just has to be meaningful and motivating to you. It has to help you show up as the Wise Leader at work with a clear direction and a clear desired outcome; whether that is to make the best widget in the world or to end world hunger is up to you. There is no right or wrong. You just have to choose. Yes, choose. I know there is a sense of our purpose being a secret, but at the end of the day, we have free-will, and we get to choose what our purpose is. You can't be wrong, because it is yours. It has to resonate in your heart, no one else's. Take the pressure off yourself of having to get it "right" or "perfect." Just choose, and if at some point it no longer feels right, choose again. Who is to say we just have one purpose or one career? It's up to you. Too many people waste years in indecision trying to get their purpose perfect. It is better to act and learn from those actions than to stay stagnant. A Wise Leader is not stagnant. A Wise Leader is always evolving.

Summary

In this chapter, we discussed what Wise Leadership looks like at work. We applied each of the 5 principles: Claim Your Leadership, Unleash Your Ambition, Find Your Voice, Lift Each Other Up, and the Power of Purpose to your work-life and career. For some of you, you may not have big ambitions in your career, and for others, you may already be sitting in the C-Suite. Regardless of where you are at or where you want to go, you can be a Wise Leader in the office by influencing others in a positive way that benefits the greater good of the work environment. Here are some ways you might begin implementing the principles at work:

- Claiming Your Leadership at Work begins with deciding that you are a leader, and then choosing to show up as one each day by the way you move, speak, dress, treat others etc...

- Unleashing Your Ambition at Work means going after what you really want. No more playing small or staying quiet. No more letting fear overcome your dreams. Now start gathering your team to help you get there.

- Finding Your Voice at Work is deciding on your leadership style. How do you want others to perceive you, describe you? While you can't control other's thoughts, nor please everyone, think about the type of leader you want to be and use your voice to represent that. Start speaking up on important issues and making decisions from a place of leadership.

- Lifting Each Other Up at Work is choosing an abundance mindset over a scarcity mindset; believing that there is enough money, prestige, leadership to go around. It's choosing collaboration over competition and celebrating your colleagues and co-workers' successes.

- <u>The Power of Purpose at Work</u> is really about knowing your WHY and knowing what your purpose is. For Wise Leaders, their work is a calling, not just a job, and they have to be strongly motivated by a mission. That mission does not have to be huge, but it has to be salient to the Wise Leader. If you don't know what your purpose is, refer back to the exercise in this chapter. But at the end of the day, don't make it a mystery. Just choose. You have free-will, and you get to decide.

For more help embodying Wise Leadership at work, go to www.drdonnamarino.com/unleash for a guided visualization to help see yourself as the Wise Leader at work.

Chapter 13: In Your Community

You may have big ambitions in your community, or you may have relatively small ambitions for your community; but we all live in one, and how we choose to show up impacts everyone in it. You can choose to be a Wise Leader in your community by running for political office, or you can choose to be a Wise Leader by being polite to others at the grocery store or picking up trash on the ground in the neighborhood. By now, you should see that Wise Leadership is as much about attitude as it is about action. There is always a way to demonstrate your Wise Leadership, no matter how big or small your ambitions. Not everyone is cut out to run for office, but we can all do our part. Imagine what a community of Wise Leaders would look and feel like. Imagine the gift that would be to yourself, your children, your neighbors. Imagine how that could change the world.

Claiming Your Leadership in your Community

Think about it for a minute. How do *you* personally want to claim your leadership in your community? What does that look and feel like for you? What would be different if you just decided that you are a Wise Leader in your community? Would you think differently? Act differently?

Perhaps you're reading these questions and thinking, "I'm already a busy working mom. I have no more time left in the day to be involved in the community as well." Or perhaps you are the President of the PTA and feel you've already claimed your leadership in the community. This is not to judge either way, but a time to reflect. We can all take on roles and titles, but not be Wise Leaders. We can also sit on the sidelines and not be a Wise Leader. This is also not about over-extending ourselves, as many women do. It's not about taking on more, but it's about attitude, and taking on the things that are meaningful to us and dropping the things that aren't.

So, if you decided today to Claim your Wise Leadership status in your community, how would you think, feel, or act differently? What would it mean to you? Perhaps you are still the President of the PTA, but you show up differently. Or you are that busy working mom, but you decide to help the elderly neighbor by doing her grocery shopping for her when you do yours. Or maybe you have big ambitions, and it's time to run for office to make real change in your community. Ultimately, you get to decide what honors your values and what creates the community you want to live in, while still allowing yourself the time to take care of you and your family. But it starts with the decision to claim it! Are you going to give yourself Wise Leader status, or are you going to stay the same?

I invite you to take some time to journal on all of these questions, or use the Wise Leader Workbook, to get really clear for yourself what would be different if you claimed your leadership in your community. How is your not claiming your leadership affecting your community? What is your responsibility as a community member? The Wise Leader who claims her leadership in the community, understands the importance of her role as a community member, and how she has the potential to influence everyone around her, even if just by a smile or her kind word.

Unleashing Your Ambition in your Community

This is a fun one, I think. Think about all the things that you have wanted to do in your community but were too afraid to before; things that you want to be different, things that you thought were someone else's job, things that were not for you because you weren't smart enough, or political enough, or didn't know the right people; things you thought maybe someday I'll... Write everything down that comes to mind. Maybe you've toyed with the idea of running for a spot on the school board or opening a local business or even just starting a book club for the neighborhood. Write it down, and instead of looking for all the reasons why you couldn't or shouldn't do it, start writing down all the reasons that you are the perfect person for the job. Remember, you're a Wise Leader now, so even if you didn't feel qualified before, you are now.

When you choose to unleash your ambition in the community as a Wise Leader, you make a positive impact. You show up with integrity. You think about how your actions affect others. You do things for the greater good, but not in a martyrdom, self-sacrificing way. You show up with an understanding that we are all in this together and that we all have a role to play in how our community treats each other, respects one another, cares for each other or not.

In fact, as I write this, we are experiencing a global pandemic, COVID-19. I am writing this as a Wise Leader from my home as I am social distancing. How am I being a Wise Leader in my community right now? Ironically, by not being in it! At the time of this writing, my family and I have been home now for months. We have only left for essential shopping. If we go for walks, we stay away from other people and even cross the street if we need to. Nothing has come into our home that has not been disinfected, and we have not been in physical contact with anyone but the people that live in this house. How is this unleashing your ambition, you might say? It is unleashing my ambition to keep my community safe, especially the most vulnerable populations such as the elderly and immuno-compromised. It is both claiming my leadership, and unleashing my ambition to be a good citizen, and help put an end to this pandemic. It is leading myself, my home, my community, and the world all in one. This is a very real and current example of how Wise Leadership works in the real world. How you can implement it on a day to day basis and how far and wide your reach is even with acts that seem so small, such as staying home.

But it is a choice. I have witnessed others, not social distancing. That is not Wise Leadership. That is not considering how your actions and attitudes impact others. Everything is a choice, and I hope that you choose wisely.

Finding Your Voice in your Community

Do you have a voice in your community? How do you express it? One way to express your voice in your community is to get out and vote. Voting at any level is your chance to be heard, whether it is your PTA election, your local government, or federal. It is an important way of expressing your voice and being a Wise Leader. I believe that voting is imperative to being a Wise Leader in your community.

How else can you find and express your voice in your community? Remember that finding your voice is about consciously choosing how you want to be seen and heard in your community. What is important to you in your community? What are your community values, and how will you express them?

A Wise Leader in the community is polite and respectful to others but speaks up when needed. She treats her grocery clerk, her waitress, and her mayor with the same dignity and respect, but is not afraid to advocate for her values and beliefs. Finding your voice in your community can range from how you speak to others at the grocery store to attending a Women's March or political rally. It might be attending a town hall meeting, a school board meeting, or a PTA event. It is advocating for your values and beliefs, but it is never disrespectful, bullying, or nasty. It is expressing yourself with integrity, kindness, and conviction for what you believe is right and just.

Finding your voice in the community can also be supporting the local businesses you appreciate and advocating for others to do the same. It could be purchasing gift cards for local businesses at the holidays. Your dollars count big in your community and are an extension of your voice.

I want you to take some time to reflect on how you have or have not been expressing your voice in your community. Also, think about where you have been expressing yourself. Have you been doing it as a Wise Leader or someone else? Where would you like to speak up more or differently? Maybe you have been advocating for your beliefs, but maybe there is a better, wiser way to do it.

Lifting Each Other Up in your Community

Can you imagine a community that was dedicated to lifting each other up? Can you imagine what that would look like and feel like? Can you imagine raising a family in that community? Isn't that what we all want? It starts with you.

In Chapter 6, we talked about the positivity ratio as it relates to fear. We discussed the negativity bias, and how our brain attaches to negativity, as part as a leftover survival mechanism, and how it takes 3-5 positive experiences to equate to just one negative experience. Now imagine that you are in the community, and someone says something nasty to you. Imagine how that makes you feel. Imagine how it can impact your day. Imagine how it impacts how you then treat others. Can you see the potential domino effect here?

Now, let's imagine that you walk around all day, making a point to compliment at least one person everywhere that you go. Imagine how that person feels when you compliment them. Imagine it's the barista handing you your coffee or the grocery bagger bagging your groceries. Imagine how that impacts their day. Imagine how it makes you feel. Can you see the domino effect there?

Every day, we get to choose how to treat others. Every day we get to choose to be a positive and kind influence in the world, or to be someone doesn't take the time to acknowledge others or, worse, takes the time to bring others down. In an individualistic society, we can sometimes forget about our impact on others. We can have a very insular view at times. The Wise Leader takes her blinders off and thinks about others. She actively works to lift them up; to go out of her way to hold a door, to say thank you, to compliment a job well done. She is aware of her potential influence on others and actively chooses to make it a positive one. That is what Wise Leadership in the community looks like. Good communities don't just happen. We either create them, or we don't.

The Power of Purpose in your Community

As you already know, a Wise Leader has to know her purpose. It is the guiding force for everything else. So what is your purpose for being a Wise Leader in the community? I think we all want to live in friendly, thoughtful, caring, and "neighborly" communities, but often we think it is someone else's job to create that. We think it's the politicians, or the other neighbors, or the rest of the community. It can feel like a foreign or abstract concept that just happens on its own. It can feel quite removed from ourselves, but it isn't. We all make it happen. We all have to choose to make it happen. It is important for you to connect with WHY you want to live in a community like that, and to see yourself as playing a major role in creating your ideal community, or else you will just sit on the sidelines. The further we move outside of our homes through those concentric circles we spoke about, the more abstract it can feel, the more lost we can feel or disconnected from the outcomes. Connecting to our WHY is what brings it all home. It's what connects the abstract (our community, or as we will talk about next, the world) to the tangible (our lives, our homes). In order for our brain to make those connections, we have to have a powerful why. We have to connect what happens in the community to what happens in our homes.

For example, I want a community that looks out for one another, especially each other's children. That is very important to me. So, how do I create that? I create it by doing things like letting the neighbors know when I spot something unusual in the neighborhood that they should look out for or by offering to drive a neighborhood kid to school when I'm driving mine because the bus didn't show up, and then just letting the mom, who is already at work, know about it. It's these actions that connect to my WHY that makes me a Wise Leader and help create the community that I desire for myself and my family.

If you don't know your WHY, you might not act. It's not always the convenient thing, after all. But what is right is not always convenient. The more powerful your why, the easier it becomes to do the right thing, and to impact positive change in your community. I encourage you to write down your WHY, and I encourage you to discuss it as a family. Talk about the kind of community you want to live in and talk about the ways your family gets to play a role in creating it. That's how we start to teach Wise Leadership in the community to our children too.

Summary

Whether you want to be the PTA president, a local politician, or just a good citizen, you can choose to show up as a Wise Leader in your community. We are all important in our community. We are all contributors. Even when we choose not to be, you are still impacting others. How we live, work, and play with others creates the communities we live in. Choosing to be a Wise Leader in your community means understanding the important role you play, and choosing to think, feel, and act towards yourself, and others in a way that represents your understanding of your potential impact, your values, your wisdom, and your respect for the community around you.

- <u>Claiming Your Leadership in the Community</u> is truly understanding your role in the community and your potential influence. It is seeing it as a responsibility. It may be your responsibility to be a good citizen, or it could be much bigger than that. Seeing yourself as a leader in your community no matter how big you desire to take that is where claiming your leadership begins.

- <u>Unleashing Your Ambition in the Community</u> can range from being that good citizen, and getting out, and voting to actually being the candidate running for political office. You get to decide how big that ambition is, but it is no longer ignoring those ambitions that have been stirring inside you for some time that you have been saying, "But, who am I to…." Now is the time to set those ambitions free, and go after what you want for your community and yourself. If the ambition is stirring inside you, it is there for a reason, and it needs to be answered.

- <u>Finding Your Voice in the Community</u> is everything from speaking a kind word to your grocery clerk, to voting, to attending a political rally. It's the best expression of your voice for your values, your beliefs, and your desire for your community. It's standing up for what you believe in, but always doing it with empathy, compassion, and respect. It is never name-calling, bullying, or unkind.

- <u>Lifting Each Other Up in the Community</u> is imperative if we want to live in positive, helpful, and kind communities. Treating each other well, saying thank you, being polite, and kind in our words, and showing appreciation for one another is the cornerstone of the types of communities we all want to raise our families in. When the Wise Leader has the opportunity to lift someone up or put someone down, she always chooses to lift.

- <u>The Power of Purpose in the Community</u> are your own personal reasons and motivations for acting as a Wise Leader in the community. They help you connect your tangible actions to the abstract of the greater good. Without knowing your WHY, it is easy to resort back to old behaviors or just an unconscious way of moving through the community. Knowing your WHY when you can't always see the full range of the impact of your actions is important fuel to keep you going and to making it all real for you.

For more help embodying Wise Leadership in the community, go to www.drdonnamarino.com/unleash for a guided visualization to help see yourself as the Wise Leader in the community.

Chapter 14: In the World

I know that there is going to be one of two reactions when getting to this chapter. There are going to be those that are saying, "yeah, right, I just want to feel successful at home, let alone the world. I'm just not that ambitious", and then there are going to be those that are saying, "YES! Let's do this!" As someone who falls into the latter category, boy can I relate to the desire to have an impact in the world, to shift paradigms, create opportunities for others, and see the world lead by conscious leadership. It simply takes my breath away at the thought. Neither reaction is right or wrong. Not everyone is called upon to lead on a global level, and that's okay. It does not make one person better than the other. The most important thing is to fulfill the level of leadership that you are called to, to stop playing small because of fear, and doubt, and to show up as the full expression of yourself in leadership, whatever that may be. We are all needed equally.

Claiming Your Leadership in the World

How does one claim their leadership in the world? Does it mean being President or some lofty title? Not necessarily. Let's start by really thinking about what do you want your impact on the world to be? What would you like to leave as your legacy? You can decide to claim your leadership in the world by saying, I am a world leader because I am raising children to be good citizens, to treat others fairly, to care about the environment, and speak against injustice. Your leadership is like throwing a stone in the water and watching the ripples expand outward. You can claim your leadership in the world by how you lead in your home, your career or in the community. Like I said before about those concentric circles, they are multidirectional.

What would happen if you decided to say to yourself, I am a World Leader? Do you chuckle? Do you reject it? How does it feel in your body? What if you redefined what it meant to be a world leader; that you didn't have to be President or Prime Minister to be one? How would you move through the world differently if you saw yourself in this way? What would you do differently?

If 'world leader' feels just too big to you, perhaps try some different words like public figure or global representative. Have some fun with this. Try on this new identity of global leadership in a fun and enthusiastic way. Think about that stone in the pond, and what you would like to ripple out from you.

Unleashing Your Ambition in the World

Now that you have claimed your global status (wink, wink), what are you going to do with it? What are your ambitions for the world around you? Think about people you know, and the impacts they have made. Who do you admire? Who would you like to be like? If nothing was stopping you if there were no limits, and you could not possibly fail, what would you do? Take some time to free write on this. Write until you've filled the front and back of three pages. If you get stuck, just wait it out until the pages are full. Perhaps, try writing one word over and over until it starts to flow again. It will take a while to break through conscious barriers and get to the subconscious that holds your deepest desires without the logical brain restricting it.

When you are done writing it, read through it, and circle all the words that jump out at you or that you find yourself having a strong emotional or physical response to. They will likely equally excite you and scare the pants off of you. My coach calls it "nercited" a combination of nervous and excited. This is when you know you are tapping into your unbridled desires and stretching your comfort zone of what your logical brain believes is possible. This is a good sign.

Just to help you get going, here are some ideas of how you might unleash your ambition in the world:

- Write a best-selling book
- Speak on stages around the world
- Host international retreats
- Start a podcast
- Be interviewed on television or a podcast
- Do a TED talk
- Run for political office
- Invent a product, service, process or technology
- Become an activist for an issue close to your heart
- Do something for the environment
- Get involved in human rights
- Travel the world, and do a good deed in every city you visit
- Teach abroad
- Create online courses for an international community
- Teach a youth group about different cultures, and religions

Honestly, the options are endless once we lay down our commonplace notions of what it means to have a global impact. When we start to open our creative minds about what that could look like, there is truly something for everyone. It is just allowing yourself the freedom of thought to tap into your deepest desires and to take action in alignment with them without your logical brain talking you out of it. We get one life to make an impact. What do you want yours to be?

Finding Your Voice in the World

You've claimed your leadership, and now you know what you want to do, so it's time to share your voice with the world. How will you go about letting others know what you are up to? Are you going to write about it? Speak about it? Record videos or podcasts?

You get to decide not only what you want to express to the world, but how you want to express it, in medium, tone, and content. We are lucky to live in a time of so many options. You can do short live videos on social media. You can write articles for online journals and magazines. You can self-publish a book or apply to speak on podcasts, television, and events. You get to choose which medium allows you to express yourself best.

You also get to choose to do it as a Wise Leader; in your authentic voice with tact, respect, and thoughtfulness. A Wise Leader uses her voice in the world for good. She knows how to get her point across and make an impact without tearing others down, name-calling, or blaming. She takes responsibility for herself and her actions. She speaks with honesty and integrity out in the world. She has her own unique way of showing up and expressing herself, but she does it with diplomacy, with intelligence, with sincerity, and of course, her wisdom. The Wise Leader uses her voice to be a light in the world, even when tackling hard or big issues. She knows that it is her light that will draw people in and help them hear her mission. She is not afraid to shine.

Lifting Each Other Up in the World

The Wise Leader knows that to lift others up is one of her greatest gifts to the world. She knows that others are more likely to do their best, be more creative, take important risks, and show up bigger when they are being lifted up than when they are being torn down. She knows that to get the best out of people, you have to show them what is possible for them.

The Wise Leader knows that people who feel genuinely good about themselves treat others well and spread the contagion of positivity.

The Wise Leader in the world compliments others, acknowledges a job well done, praises effort, and highlights others' strengths, not weaknesses.

The Wise Leader gives credit where credit is due and is focused on others more than him/herself. That does not mean that the Wise Leader neglects herself. Not at all, but it does mean that the Wise Leader is more concerned with lifting others up than patting herself on the back. She has enough confidence and self-esteem to know that she is doing good work. As the leader, she knows it's her job to make sure that others know that they are too.

When a Wise Leader does have to correct or challenge others, she does it in a way that teaches and is constructive, never tearing someone down. As a leader, she knows it's her job not just to say positive things, but to help others grow. She is a teacher, a guide, a role model, and an advisor. Her job is to help others do better, be better, and become Wise Leaders themselves.

The Power of Purpose in the World

To show up on a global level, you better have a strong WHY. The farther you expand your reach, the stronger your WHY must be. When you choose to show up in a big way, you invite others to pay attention. Some of that attention will be positive, some will be negative, and some will just ignore you. You have to have a strong foundation to return to when it gets hard.

Being a Wise Leader in the world means raising your level of visibility, which many people struggle with. If your desire is not bigger than your fear, you will shrink back to old ways. Your desire is your WHY. The more you stretch, the more the fear monster raises its ugly head. Your WHY is your ammunition against the fear monster.

Make sure you get very clear on WHY you want to be a bestselling author or a public figure or enter into politics or take up a cause, whatever it is for you. Know it in your heart. Write it down. Write down every reason you can think of and make it *emotional*. Humans make decisions from emotion. As much as we want to think we are logical, it is emotion that gets us to take risks, to be visible, and to go after what we want. Logic will have us playing safe in the corner every time. If your WHY does not stir you emotionally, then it is not good enough, and you will not be willing to take the risks you need to have a global impact. If you want to be a Wise Leader in the World, have a big, juicy WHY.

Summary

Being a Wise Leader in the World may not be for everyone, and that is okay. You might not be ready for this concept yet, or you may be dying to jump right in. You can always come back to this chapter later if you need to. Just remember that you get to define your impact and your legacy. Every pebble tossed into the water leaves a ripple, so you are making an impact in the world whether you are ready to claim it or not.

- Claiming Your Leadership in the World means deciding for yourself what it means to be a wise leader in the world. Is that something you can own? What would it look and feel like if you did? What would be different? Perhaps you can let go of old notions of what a world leader is and create a definition that you are ready to claim.

- Unleashing Your Ambition in the World can range from educating others on global issues to running for political office. There are so many ways to show up in the world. What is your unique gift that you want to share with others? Is it writing a book? Speaking on stages? Teaching online? What is your heart's desire if you had no limits? What is the legacy you want to leave? That is what you need to unleash in the world.

- Finding Your Voice in the World means you get to choose your message, your medium, and your tone. You get to decide how you want to be known for how you express yourself and how you speak to others. Wise Leaders use their authentic voice to make a positive impact in the world. They choose to be a light that draws others in. They are not afraid to shine.

- Lifting Each Other Up in the World is one of the greatest gifts of being a Wise Leader in the world. The Wise Leader knows that others will show up as the best version of themselves when they are respected, appreciated, and acknowledged. She knows that to get the best out of people, you have to show them what is possible for them. She knows that this is her primary task and the gateway to her positive impact in the world.

- The Power of Purpose in the World is your most important WHY. Without a big, juicy WHY, it is going to be very challenging to show up on a global level. It is very important that you are not only clear on your WHY, but that it is also highly emotionally charged. Your WHY has to be greater than all of your fears of going after it.

For more help embodying Wise Leadership in the world, go to www.drdonnamarino.com/unleash for a guided visualization to help see yourself as the Wise Leader in the world.

Chapter 15: Why you need to put this book into action NOW: A Plea

As I am completing this book, we are in the midst of the COVID-19 Pandemic. Half a million people in the US are sick, and we have had over 17,000 deaths. During the time it took me to write the last chapter, 250 people died. The United States, one of the richest countries in the world, has more cases than anywhere else in the world. The state of New York alone has surpassed Italy and Spain in the number of confirmed cases. We are living in an unprecedented time where Wise Leadership is needed now more than ever.

I believe the birth of Wise Leadership is the pathway to justice, innovation, compassion, and global change. I believe it is how we get to conscious capitalism, conscious consumerism, and conscious living. It is how we all rise to better versions of ourselves by lifting one another up, allowing the flow, and exchange of ideas, and bringing more diversity to the leadership table.

As of January 30, 2020, the Council on Foreign Relations reported that only 19 out of 193 countries have a female head of state or government, only nine countries have at least 50% women in the national cabinet, and only four countries have at least 50% women in the national legislature. Why is this important to Wise Leadership? Because studies show that women are more likely to reach across party lines, and they pass more legislation. In other words, they get things done by working together! They are also more likely to challenge established conventions and political agendas. Challenging convention is how we remain current with the times, but it is also how we innovate. Innovation is what brings us solutions such as: vaccines, technology, new ways of working remotely, etc...

Now more than ever, we need to work together on a global level. We need to be conscious of our impact on others, not just in our homes and our communities, but in the world. We need people to voice their concerns, their ideas, and their contributions. We need people to show up and to be heard. We need YOU!

What we don't need is more bullying, name-calling, and big egos getting in the way of what is right. We don't need leaders who are more worried about their position or their wallets than the people they are supposed to serve. We don't need more of the same. We need something completely different.

We need Wise Leaders who lead from a place of values, integrity, honesty, and compassion. We need collaboration, not competition. We need people who are working for the highest good *of all*. Leaders who can acknowledge their strengths and weaknesses and can delegate to those that can do it better than them because they are more worried about getting things done right than they are their own egos. We need a world where we look out for one another, where we understand just how far and wide our actions can ripple out and affect other's lives, and where we each take responsibility for that ripple.

What if we all lived that way? What if we were lead that way? If you feel the calling to be a Wise Leader, at home, at the office, in your community or in the world, I hope you answer it because we need you. Now more than ever.

Much Love,
Dr. Donna

NOTE: Between the completion of this book and its publishing, the number of cases of COVID-19 in the U.S. has risen to over 6.6 million, with over 197,000 deaths in just six and a half months.

In the past seven days, nearly 6,000 people died (997 just yesterday) from COVID-19 in the U.S.

New Zealand, one of the 14 female-led countries, lost only one soul in that same week. We need you!

Made in the USA
Monee, IL
28 September 2020